Bahamian Cooking & Menus

with Jerk, Barbecue and Selected Menus

By
**Master Chef
Leonard 'Sonny' Henry**
and
Mike Henry

LMH Publishing

© 1999 Mike Henry
9 8 7 6 5 4 3 2 1

All rights reserved. No part of this book may be reproduced, stored in a retrieval system, or transmitted, in any form or by any means, electronic, mechanical, photocopying, recording, or otherwise, without the prior written permission of the publishers or author.

The publishers have made every effort to trace the copyright holders but if they have inadvertently overlooked any, they will be pleased to make the necessary arrangements at the first opportunity.

If you have bought this book without a cover you should be aware that it is "stolen" property. The publishers/author have not received any payment for the "stripped" book, if it is printed without their authorization.

Published by LMH Publishing Ltd.
7-9 Norman Road, Kingston CSO
Email: henryles@cwjamaica.com

Printed & Bound in Jamaica

ISBN 976-610-168-X

CONTENTS

FOREWORD iv
INTRODUCTION TO BAHAMIAN FOOD v
MEET THE FAMILY ISLANDERS vi
APPETIZERS AND HORS D'OEVURES 1
SOUPS 5
FISH AND SHELLFISH 10
POULTRY 16
MEATS 22
VEGETABLES 28
SALADS 35
DRESSINGS AND SAUCES 40
BARBECUES 44
PICKLES AND PRESERVES 52
JELLIES AND JAMS 56
DESSERTS 59
CAKES AND BREADS 65
BEVERAGES 71
MENUS 74
GLOSSARY OF COOKING TERMS 78
35 USEFUL COOKING AND
    HOUSEHOLD HINTS 80
TABLE OF MEASUREMENTS AND
    MISCELLANEOUS EQUIVALENTS 82
SOME SUBSTITUTIONS 82
QUANTITIES PER HEAD 83
USEFUL KITCHEN EQUIPMENT 83
INDEX 84

Foreword

This is a cookbook devoted to people who delight in tasty, spicy food. The special sections on Barbecues and Menus will be a helpful aid to those who enjoy summer entertaining. The index also makes the book a useful reference for those interested in serious cuisine.

The recipes in the book reflect to a large extent the cultural heritage of the people of the Bahamas: thus you will find many of the dishes use the food we grow, such as peas, coconut, paw-paw, mango, okra and many others, which are considered exotic in other parts of the world.

For our foreign visitors who wish to prepare at home some of the dishes they may have tasted in restaurants or hotels, this book will be a handy guide. In many cases they will be able to find the ingredients they need in their local markets or West Indian communities.

For those who live here, may this book encourage a new and happy familiarity with our own cooking.

The Publishers

A SHORT INTRODUCTION TO BAHAMIAN FOOD

FISH

In the teeming blue waters of the 700 islands of the Bahamas, fish is plentiful and has historically been a means of support to much of the population. Fish to sell, fish for fun and fish for the pot. No matter how we get it, fish is on a Bahamian table more often than any meat.

SHELLFISH

Conch

Perhaps other than the natural beauty, nothing is more synonymous with the Bahamas than the 'Conch', known as the giant of the ocean without a bone. The Conch's home is a multi-coloured shell; and its remarkable strength enables it to suck tightly into its shell, so that neither man nor fish can pull it out. Throughout history, the Bahamians have used conch for food; removing the conch from its shell either by crushing or breaking into the pointed end of the shell and cutting the conch away with a knife. The shell is often used for home or garden decoration, or as land fill.

Out Islands Conch

Because of its winding chain of islands connected only by the sea; the innovations of the Bahamian plays an important role, any Island other than Nassau is known as the out islands and as the name implies, this is their way to prepare Conch. After the conch is taken from its shell, it is bruised, flattened and tenderized then hung in the sun to be cured. Day by day the colour changes until the texture of conch becomes like that of ham. After being cured, the meat is usually good for at least a year. Preparing conch this way is usally done before the hurricane season when bad weather may prevent the Bahamian out islanders from travelling to the capital (Nassau) to purchase other meats. Conch prepared this way is used for chowder and fritters. But, the conch then needs to soak in water overnight before preparing; after which it is either boiled or tenderized before making chowder or ground to make fritters. Reason enough for the Bahamian to call Conch done this way "Hurricane Ham...

It is a widely-held belief that the conch is an aphrodisiac and the older Bahamians still prepare a special tonic made from the drippings of the fresh conch, rich in vitamins and iron.

Crawfish

From the same azure waters of the Bahamas Islands and taking pride of place on any menu, is the snow white meat of the 'crawfish' a delectable and tasty shellfish known to satisfy the most varied tastes.

Cousin to the Maine Lobster, with two feelers instead of claws, crawfish meat is a little tighter but with true Bahamian artistry, crawfish can be prepared to equal any lobster from Maine.

Whether you roast it, bake it, boil it, push it, mince it, stew it, steam it, or make a salad of it, crawfish is sure to please the most discriminating palate.

VEGETABLES

Pigeon Pea

In the world of vegetables the Pigeon Pea is very popular throughout the Bahamas Islands, planted in almost every back yard from Grand Bahama to Inauga. A stroll around the wharf in Nassau during Christmas time gives the non-Bahamian a chance to see and feel the importance of this home-grown pea. When dried and boiled as the Bahamians do, the water becomes dark brown. The pea and its water is used to cook 'peas and rice', soup, and other recipes. The water from the pea gives the flavour and abounds with iron. Need we say more than ask you to try a meal of "Peas and Rice" and "Conch Salad".

Fresh Okra

This vegetable may be prepared in many ways, and in the skilled hands of a Bahamian cook is most tasty and nourishing. Today, some of the recipes are considered old fashioned, but to the gourmet and the experimental diner 'okra' is a delight.

POULTRY

White Crown Pigeon

This game bird of the Bahamas, is a must to those who know about them, and not too many visitors seem to know about them.

The white crown pigeon starts to scout the Islands around March to select its nesting and feeding grounds. When it has completed its survey of the prime areas for food, water and privacy, the white crown disappears to return a couple of weeks later.

It is at this point that the hunters (bird shooters) who themselves have observed the habits of the white pigeon arrive for the bird season and with skill and marksmanship bring home this delectable meat to grace the Bahamian table.

All in all, this is a mere sample of Bahamian cooking ingredients presenting a new approach to good food and exciting dishes from Appetizers to Desserts – Bon appetit!

WHILE YOU COOK
MEET THE FAMILY OF ISLANDERS

ABACO

Site of the Hope Town lighthouse and where the blue waters teem with the National Fish, the Blue Marlin, also home of the Abaco Wild Hog. (Recipe page 25). Located here also is the third largest Bahamian settlement, Marsh Harbour. While there, please pay a visit to "Conch Inn or the Hope Town Lodge Restaurant" and you will savour the finest Bahamian cuisine.

ANDROS

The big Island three-fourths the size of Puerto Rico and an "in" resort, a fisherman's dream of crabs and conch; and a safe bet that many of the recipes you enjoy are made with the catch from Andros. Certainly a shooter's paradise when he hunts for the White Crown Pigeon (recipe page 18), a delicacy of memorable taste.

BIMINI
A pictorial paradise of beauty, the place where Ernest Hemmingway made his second home; and ate at his favourite restaurant, "The Complete Angler", still there for you to enjoy.

LUCAYA
Home of the Dolphin and an area renowned for its sunken treasures, real and imaginary. But there is nothing imaginary about the culinary artistry of the cooks from this Island.

EXUMA
An Island known as "the sailor's shangrilla"

FREEPORT
As the name implies, a treasure trove of fine shopping, exotic architectural and sophisticated restaurants, serving the finest Bahamian cuisine.

ELUETHERA
Where the sand takes on the romantic colour of pink, lending charm and ambiance to 18th century villages, and where the juciest pineapples this side of heaven are produced, that's what we used in the Pineapple Jam recipe (page 56).

NEW PROVIDENCE
With its bustling capital Nassau, this Island is known as the Scotland of the tropics, where golf and good food abond.

GREEN TURTLE CAY
As the name implies, this food of the Gods abound and it's used to create those mouthwatering recipes on page 9.

CAT ISLAND
This delightful Island boasts the highest point in the Bahamas. Mount Alvernia rises some 206 feet into the sky.

LONG ISLAND
Here on this charming Island, the Bahamian farmer raises the finest sheep. (Try our Barbecued Lamp Chops, recipe on page 46).

SAN SALVADOR
The first landing place of Columbus in 1492 and perhaps where he discovered the Amerindians whose staple food once was the Jamaican hutias which also exists in Bahamas and is now an endangered species.

INAGUA
Here on this beautiful Island reside the National Bird of the Bahamas, the beautiful Flamingoes and where the pigeon pea is grown.

Appetizers & Hors d'oeuvres

OYSTERS

The best way to eat fresh oysters is raw. Open the oysters and lay on a bed of crushed ice. Dress with lime juice. Brown bread and butter is usually served.

CRAWFISH CURRY

2 cups crawfish, cooked, shredded and chilled
½ cup mayonnaise
¼ teaspoon curry powder
2 teaspoons onion, minced
2 teaspoons lemon juice

Place crawfish in a mixing bowl. Mix together remaining ingredients and combine with the crawfish. Serve on assorted crackers..

EGG PLANT ELEGANTE
(garden egg)

1 peeled egg plant
2 boiled crushed potatoes
* salt, pepper, flour, oil
* chopped garlic (1 clove)
* vinegar and oil

Slice garden egg lengthwise into fingers. Season with salt and pepper and roll in flour. Drop into deep hot oil and fry until crisp.

Combine crushed potatoes, garlic and enough vinegar and oil to make a paste of dipping consistency. Place in a bowl and use fried egg plant fingers as scoops.

GRAPEFRUIT WITH SHRIMP AND SOUR CREAM

½ grapefruit per person
6 shrimps, cooked and cleaned per person

1 cup sour cream
1 tablespoon mayonnaise

Cut grapefruit in half. Core and remove pulp. Discard seeds.
Fill with cooked shrimps, marinated in sour cream and mayonnaise and mixed with grapefruit pulp.

PINEAPPLE APPETIZER

* pieces of fresh pineapple
* cream cheese

* chopped cashew nuts

Dip pieces of pineapple in cheese and roll in cashews.

COCONUT CHIPS

1 dry coconut

Remove meat from shell. Cut meat into thin strips and arrange in a shallow pan. Sprinkle with salt and roast in a slow oven. Stir occasionally.

FRIED PLANTAIN CHIPS

1 green plantain

* oil

Peel plantain and cut into thick slices. Fry in hot oil. Drain on paper towel. Sprinkle with salt to serve.

PORK (RIND)

* whatever quantity desired
2-3 tablespoon oil

* salt

Cut rind (skin) into small pieces and fry until crisp in oil. Sprinkle with salt.

CRAWFISH FRITTERS

3 to 4 medium crawfish tails
1 medium onion, finely chopped
3 tablespoons baking powder
   chopped
2 cups flour
2 cups water
2 hot peppers
2 teaspoons salt
1 stalk celery, finely chopped
cooking oil

Boil crawfish tails for three quarters of an hour and allow to cool. Remove meat from shell, cut very fine. Pour all ingredients including crawfish into a bowl. Mix until a smooth mixture is obtained. This should be fairly thick. Drop ½ teaspoonful at a time into a pan of hot fat and fry until golden brown.

NASSAU CAKE

4 tomatoes
2 sweet peppers
3 green or black olives
1 tablespoon chopped onion
* oil, salt, pepper
1 french type loaf of bread

(Make this the day before it is to be used.)

Chop tomatoes, peppers and olives. Add onion and seasoning. Cut bread in half lengthwise. Remove the crumbs and mix them into the tomato mixture, kneading it with a little oil, salt and pepper.

Fill the bread halves, and press together. Wrap in foil and refrigerate. Cut in slices to serve.

PEPPER SHRIMPS

1 pint of shrimps
* white vinegar, water
* sliced hot pepper (remove the seeds)
½ sliced onion
* salt and pimento grains

Cover shrimps with salted water and boil until tender. Cool, peel and clean them. Meanwhile mix vinegar, peppers, onions and pimento grains. Bring to a boil. Pour over shrimps and store in a covered jar for 12 hours before serving .

CRAWFISH BITS

2 lbs. crawfish tails
   cooked and cut into
   1 inch pieces
   Pepper to taste
½ cup butter or margarine
Garlic salt or plain salt to taste

Pan broil crawfish pieces in butter or margarine and seasonings, turning occasionally unitl lightly browned. Serve with dip of your choice or try a mixture of catsup and horseraddish.

WATER MELON MARBLES

1 water melon
¼ pint rum
2 oranges

2 tablespoons sugar
* cherries

Cut the melon in half lengthwise. Remove the seeds, then with a ball-scoop remove the flesh of the melon. The shell can be kept to be a serving dish if wished.

Place the melon balls in a bowl. Mix the rum, orange juice and sugar together and pour over the melon balls. Refrigerate for at least one hour.

To serve, place a cocktail stick in each ball and pile up on a bed of cracked ice in the melon shell.

CRAWFISH DIP

1 medium crawfish tail, cooked and cut in pieces
1 package (8 ounces) cream cheese, softened

½ teaspoon Tabasco
¼ cup dry white wine
dash of salt

Boil or steam crawfish in 1 cup water for 15 to 20 minutes or until done. Remove flesh (meat) from shell and central vein. Place all ingredients in a small baking dish and stir together. Place in heated oven at 350°F for 15 minutes or until very hot. Serve with crackers, carrot sticks or raw cauliflower bulbs.

SEASONED BREADFRUIT CHIPS WITH AVOCADO CREAM CHEESE DIP

Breadfruit Chips
1 breadfruit
* salt
* black pepper

* onion salt
* garlic powder
* oil

Peel breadfruit, cut into sections and remove the heart. Cut into slices and place in salted water for half an hour or more. Dry the slices and fry in hot fat until golden. Drain on paper towels. Meanwhile, mix the salt and seasonings together and sprinkle over the chips just before serving.

Avocado Cream Cheese Dip
1 medium avocado pear
6 ozs. cream cheese
½ teaspoon minced onion

1 tablespoon lemon or lime juice
2 tablespoons milk
* salt

Halve avocado lengthwise and remove seed. Scoop out the pulp. The shell can be saved to be used as a container for serving, otherwise discard. Mash the pulp with cream cheese and other ingredients. Serve piled in a small dish or the shell, surrounded by breadfruit chips.

BAHAMIAN CONCH SOUP

- 1 cup of cooked and chopped conch meat which has been boiled in 1 qrt. of water
- ½ lb. diced tomatoes
- * only meat of young Queen conch to be used
- ½ lb. sliced onions
- 2 tablespoons oil
- * herbs, garlic, salt to taste
- * sherry optional

Heat oil and fry onions, tomatoes, and seasonings. Add these ingredients to conch meat and liquid. Cook about 20 minutes.

1 teaspoon sherry is often added to this.

OKRA SOUP

- 2 lbs. meat – beef and mutton
- 2 qts. water
- 2 tablespoons salt
- 3 large ripe tomatoes
- 2 dozen okras, finely cut up
- 1 onion chopped
- ¼ cabbage, cut up
- 2 tablespoons cooking oil
- pepper to taste
- ½ teaspoon thyme
- 2 tablespoons flour
- 1 stalk celery, cut up

Boil meats and cabbage until tender. Heat cooking oil in frying pan. Add flour and allow to brown. Add okras, onions, celery and tomatoes and continue to cook for about 5 minutes on a low heat. Pour the mixture onto the boiled meats. Add thyme, salt and pepper and boil for a further 15 minutes. Corn, carrots, potatoes or other vegetables may be added but must boil in the soup until done.

COLD THICK CUCUMBER SOUP

- ½ cup diced cucumber
- ¾ cup diced cooked chicken
- 1 cup diced and cooked lobster meat
- ¼ cup chopped onion
- 1 cup milk
- 2 tablespoons sour cream
- * salt, pepper, parsley

Mix the milk into the sour cream and thin down. Add all other ingredients. Chill for 2 hours before serving.

COCKEREL SOUP

4 lb. cockerel (a young cock)
2 qrts. water
2 sliced carrots
2 sliced potatoes
* onion, thyme, salt and a hot pepper

Boil the cockerel in water. When tender, strain and skim. Add vegetables, seasonings, and strips of the meat to the liquid.

Boil until vegetables are tender. Water may be added if it has boiled away.

Remove the hot pepper without breaking it in the cooking liquid.

CRAB SOUP

6 crabs, preferably white
1 stalk celery, chopped
1 teaspoon thyme
2 tablespoons cooking oil
1 onion, sliced
½ green pepper, sliced
2 cups cooked pigeon peas
milk from two coconuts

Clean crabs, remove fat and set aside with bodies. Pour cooking oil into frying pan. Fry onion, green pepper and celery until soft. Stir tomato paste, crab fat and bodies and allow to steam for 10 minutes. Add pigeon peas and coconut milk, season to taste. Boil for a further 10 minutes. Prepare dumplings by mixing 1½ cups of flour, 1 teaspoon of salt and ¾ cup water together. Knead thoroughly. Roll out dough and cut into dumplings. Place the dumplings into soup stir and allow dumplings to cook about 10 minutes. Cooked salt beef may be added if desired.

BEET SOUP

8 large cooked and peeled beetroot
1 lb. soup meat cut into cubes
3 diced tomatoes
2 qrts. water
1 cup shredded cabbage
* salt, pepper
* sour cream

Combine meat, tomatoes and water in a saucepan. Bring to a boil. Skim and cook for about an hour.

Add the cabbage, salt, and pepper. Cook for 30 minutes.

Grate the beetroots and add to the soup with salt and pepper. Cook for 15 minutes.

Serve very hot, with a spoonful of sour cream and a few pieces of the meat in each soup bowl.

WHELK SOUP

2 cups whelk removed from shells and cleaned
6 cups water
1 stalk celery, finely chopped
½ medium sweet pepper
2 medium potatoes, diced
1 cup noodles, uncooked
8 cups water
1 small onion finely chopped

Put whelk meat through meat grinder. Place in cooking pot with 6 cups water. Parboil for approximately 1–1½ hours; drain. Add celery, sweet pepper, onion, potato, noodles, tomato paste, seasoning and 8 cups water. Cook until potato is tender.

FISH CHOWDER

2 lbs. of any type of white fish meat
1 qrt. water
1 minced onion
2 diced carrots
1 diced potato
2 diced tomatoes
* salt and pepper to taste
* sherry, optional

Boil fish in water until tender. Remove all bones and strain the liquid. Stir diced vegetables into fish stock with seasonings. When cooked add some flaked fish meat and sherry to taste.

ISLAND FISH TEA

3 lbs. of fish cut into pieces
6 cups water
2 chopped onions
2 chopped tomatoes
1 hot pepper
1 tsp. thyme
* squeeze of lime juice

Place all ingredients in a pot with water. Bring to the boil and simmer gently for about an hour.
Strain off liquid and serve with chopped parsley.

SPLIT PEA SOUP

2 cups yellow split peas
1 teaspoon salt
3 stalks celery, sliced
2 large onions, diced
3 large potatoes, peeled and quartered
5 cups water
1 teaspoon thyme
2 large carrots, peeled and sliced
1 lb. meat — salt beef may be used
(soaked overnight)

If using salt beef, soak in water mixed with vinegar overnight. Wash peas, soak in 5 cups water overnight, drain. Add salt to water (if using fresh beef), bring to a boil. Add peas, lower heat. Simmer about ½ hour or until tender. Puree peas through sieve or blender. While peas cook, place meat into a pot. Add thyme and cook about 1½ hours, then add celery, carrots, onion and potatoes and cook 30 minutes longer. Remove meat and vegetables from broth. Stir broth into pureed peas and simmer until thick. Add cooked vegetables to soup.

GUNGU OR COW PEA SOUP

1 pint of peas (soaked overnight)
2 qrts. water
1 lb. soup meat
1 sliced coco
1 chopped onion
* thyme, salt, pepper

Boil peas with soup meat in water until tender. Remove the meat and put peas through a colander, rub out and discard skin.
Place liquid on stove with seasonings and coco. Add more water if necessary.
When coco is cooked and dissolved, the soup is ready. Bits of the boiled meat can be added.

PAW PAW (PAPAYA) SOUP

2 tablespoons butter
1 sliced onion
1 paw paw peeled, seeded and sliced – use a fruit which is past the green stage but not yet ripe

3 cups water
* a sprig of parsley
* salt, pepper and a dash of nutmeg
3 cups milk
1 tablespoon cornstarch

Melt butter and fry onions. Add the paw paw, water, parsley, salt and pepper. Cover and boil over a low heat for about one hour, or until paw paw is tender enough to force through a sieve.

Return to saucepan and add nutmeg. Mix cornstarch into milk until smooth, and add to the paw paw mixture. Stir, constantly.

Cook for 10 minutes more over low heat, but do not allow to boil.

PEPPER POT

2 lbs. of chopped callaloo or spinach
2 qrts. water
1 lb. soup meat
2 slices bacon or a pig's tail
1 lb. pre-cooked shrimp

1 doz. okras sliced
1 minced onion
1 diced coco
* salt, pepper, herbs, hot pepper to taste

Place meat and bacon in a soup pot with water. Boil until meat is tender.

Add callaloo, okras, coco and seasonings. Simmer until soup has thickened.

Remove hot pepper and meat (or may be left in if desired). Small flour dumplings (optional) and the shrimps are added. Simmer for 15 minutes longer.

PUMPKIN SOUP

2 lbs. pumpkin
2 qrts. water
1 lb. soup meat
* a small piece of salt pork

3 pieces chopped escallion
1 chopped coco
* thyme, salt, hot pepper

Place meat and salt pork in water and boil until meat is tender. Remove the meats.

Add peeled diced pumpkin, seasonings and chopped coco. Boil until vegetables are dissolved.

Taste for seasoning. Press through a colander and heat to serve.

CRAWFISH SOUP

1 10 oz. can cream of shrimp soup
¼ cup milk
1 cup lobster meat
1 cup shredded cheddar cheese

2 teaspoons lime juice
Dash paprika
Dash white pepper
2 teaspoons sherry

Combine first two ingredients. Cover and heat over medium heat, stir often, add remaining ingredients, except sherry. Heat to serving temperature. Stir in sherry before serving.

PIGEON PEAS SOUP AND DUMPLINGS

1 package pigeon peas
1 onion sliced
1 stalk celery, sliced
salt and pepper to taste
1 gallon water
1 tomato, diced
2 lbs. salt beef
½ green pepper sliced
1 teaspoon thyme

Soak salt beef in water mixed with vinegar overnight. Remove salt beef from water in which it has been soaking and boil in fresh water until tender. Meanwhile, place peas on to boil in a seperate pot for 2 hours or until soft. Add onion, celery, green pepper, thyme, tomato and already cooked salt beef. Boil for ½ hour. Season to taste. Mix dough with 1 cup flour, ½ cup water and ½ teaspoon salt. Knead dough, roll out thin and cut into blocks. Add dough to soup and cook for ½ hour with the pot covered.

SURPRISE TURTLE SOUP

2 lbs. stewing turtle
1 large onion, sliced
½ sweet pepper, sliced
2 tablespoons flour
1 tablespoon tomato paste
½ lb. salt pork
1 stalk celery, chopped
3 tablespoons cooking oil
1 ripe tomato, diced
salt to taste

Scald calopy and fin of turtle. Remove outside skin. Boil turtle with salt pork, onion, celery, sweet pepper and salt until meat is done. Pour cooking oil into frying pan, add flour and allow to brown. Add tomato paste and continue to steam down. Add cooked turtle and the broth. Season to taste. Boil for 10 minutes longer. Add peeled and cut up vegetables if desired.

CLEAR TURTLE SOUP

3 lbs. of turtle meat
3 qrts. of water
3 diced carrots
2 diced onions
* salt – thyme – 6 pimento grains
* lime peel – a pinch of sage
* sherry to taste

Set all ingredients except lime peel and sage to boil for about 3 hours. One hour before straining, add a piece of lime peel, and some sage. Strain through a fine sieve.
Add some sherry and pieces of the turtle meat when serving.

Variation:

THICK TURTLE SOUP

This is prepared in the same way as Clear Turtle Soup, except that it is thickened with 1 oz. of cornflour mixed with a little liquid for every qrt. of the soup.

Fish & Shellfish

BOILED FISH

- 2 lbs. any preferred fish
  salt and pepper to taste
- 2 tablespoons butter or margarine
- 2 tablespoons hot sauce
- 2 onions, sliced
  Juice of 2 lemons or limes

Place cleaned and washed fish in cooking pot and three-quarters cover with water. Add salt, pepper, butter or margarine, hot sauce and lemon juice. Place onions on top of fish and cook over medium heat until fish is tender. Avoid cooking too long as fish will flake.

BOILED CRAWFISH

- 4 boiled and cleaned crawfish tails (10–12 oz. each)
- 2 teaspoons butter
- ½ teaspoon salt
- 1 clove garlic, chopped fine
- 1 teaspoon onion, chopped fine
- 2/3 cup mayonnaise
- 2/3 cup ketchup
- 1 teaspoon mustard
- 1 oz. lime juice
- 1 oz. beer

Mince crawfish and put aside. Using a shallow pot, over medium heat, cook onion, garlic and salt in butter until onion is tender. Add ketchup, mayonnaise, mustard and beer. Add crawfish, stir and cool long enough to heat crawfish through. Add lemon juice, stir and serve.

CONCH FRITTERS

- 1 lb. raw minced conch meat
- 1 minced onion
- 4 ozs. flour
- 1 egg
- * salt, pepper
- 2 tablespoons dry breadcrumbs
- * milk and fat as needed

Mix conch meat, onion, flour, egg and seasoning together and moisten with a little milk. Shape into flat fritters. Dip in breadcrumbs and fry quickly in hot oil.

BANANA KING FISH WITH MUSTARD SAUCE

4 king fish steaks
2 ripe bananas
4 slices Cheddar cheese

* salt
* pepper
* butter

Season the fish steaks with salt and pepper. Fry gently in butter.

Place the steaks in a heat-proof dish. Cover each steak with slices of ripe banana and top with a slice of cheddar cheese. Broil until the cheese is melted and the banana heated through. Serve with mustard sauce.

Mustard Sauce

4 tablespoons mayonnaise
4 tablespoons vinegar
4 tablespoons salad oil

1 teaspoon lime juice
3 teaspoons dry mustard
* salt and pepper to taste

Mix all ingredients until smooth.

BAKED BLACK CRABS

6 black crabs, boiled
1 oz. butter, softened
½ teaspoon black pepper
1 tablespoon chopped onion
1 country pepper, finely chopped

1 teaspoon vinegar
* salt
* breadcrumbs
* butter

Clean the crabs and pick out all the meat, including the claws and smaller bones. Save four shells.

Mix the crab meat with the butter, onion, pepper, salt and vinegar. The mixture should be moist but not soggy.

Wash the shells well and wipe with a little oil. Fill each with the crab mixture, top with the breadcrumbs and dot with butter. Bake in a hot oven until the crumbs are brown.

SHELL FISH CURRY

1 – 1½ cups crawfish
1 – 1½ cups shrimp
3 medium tomatoes, peeled
1 fresh coconut, grated
1 fresh ginger root, minced
½ teaspoon brown sugar

1 qrt. milk scalded
1 – 1½ tablespoons margarine
1 large onion minced
1 clove garlic, minced
2 tablespoons fresh curry powder
2 tablespoons flour

Shell fish is to be already diced and cooked. Add grated coconut meat to the scalded milk, and let stand 1 hour. Strain through cheese cloth and squeeze until the meat is dry.

Melt butter or margarine in saucepan, add minced onion, garlic and ginger; saute lightly until onion is very light brown; add curry powder and sugar. Mix well; add flour and stir. Gradually add the milk mixture, stirring with a whisk. Place in double boiler and simmer 30 minutes. Add tomatoes, crawfish and shrimp; heat through, about 10 minutes, and serve hot.

OVEN FRIED FISH

2 lbs. of favourite fish
1 teaspoon salt
4 tablespoons butter or margarine, melted
1 cup milk
1 cup fine bread crumbs

Cut fish into serving pieces. Add salt to milk and mix well. Dip fish in milk and roll in bread crumbs; place in a well greased shallow baking dish in single layer. Pour melted butter or margarine over the fish. Place on top shelf of very hot oven (500°F.). Bake 10 to 12 minutes or until fish flakes easily with a fork. Serve immediately.

CRAB FRITTERS

½ lb. cooked crab meat (use local black crabs)
2 tablespoons oil
1 tablespoon chopped onion
3 eggs
1 tablespoon minced parsley
* breadcrumbs, salt, pepper to taste

Add onion, seasoning and beaten egg to crab meat. Add enough breadcrumbs to bind mixture. Shape into fritters and fry lightly.

ESCOVEITCH OF GROUPER

* sliced grouper fish
* oil
1 cup vinegar
2 sliced onions
2 tablespoons water
1 chopped hot pepper
* a pimento leaf and a pinch of salt

Fry fish in hot oil and set aside. Mix remaining ingredients together and bring to a boil. Simmer 20 minutes.

Lay fish in a shallow dish. Cover with hot vinegar sauce and marinate for about 12 hours before serving.

(In Mexico the fish is not cooked, it is marinated and eaten raw.)

KING FISH IN COCONUT CREAM

2 lbs. fish steaks
3 ozs. butter or margarine
1 cup coconut cream
* salt, pepper
* lime slices

Heat butter and fry steaks until brown on both sides.
To make coconut cream, grate a coconut, add water, squeeze and strain out cream. Discard pulp.
Add to fish steaks with salt and pepper.
Simmer for about 3 minutes. Garnish with lime slices.

CRAWFISH NEWBURG

2 cups crawfish, cooked and diced	½ teaspoon salt
2 tablespoons lime juice	¼ teaspoon pepper
3 tablespoons butter or margarine	2 egg yolks, well beaten
1 can (14 oz) evaporated milk	1 teaspoon sherry

Sprinkle lime juice over crawfish and set aside for 10 minutes. Put butter or margarine in saucepan, add crawfish and cook 5 minutes over low heat. Slowly stir in milk, salt and pepper, heat to boiling. Add egg yolks and cook for 2 minutes longer. Add sherry just before serving.

STEAMED CRAWFISH

Split crawfish in half lengthwise and remove central vein. Place in saucepan with lightly fitting cover with just enough salted boiling water to cover the bottom of the pan. Cover and steam until crawfish is white and tender — usually 10 – 20 minutes. Serve with lemon butter or melted butter and lemon slices.

FRIED CRAWFISH

6 medium crawfish, uncooked	½ teaspoon pepper
2 eggs	1 cup flour
½ cup evaporated milk	Oil for frying
½ teaspoon salt	Butter or margarine
Lemon juice	

Beat eggs and milk together. Add salt and pepper. Dip crawfish thoroughly in egg-milk mixture, then roll in flour. Have hot fat about ½ inch deep in heavy frying pan and cook until golden brown, turning once. Serve with melted lemon butter.

LOBSTER CREOLE

2 lbs. cooked and shredded lobster meat	3 diced tomatoes
2 chopped onions	2 tablespoons rum or sherry
2 chopped sweet peppers	4 tablespoons oil
	* salt, pepper, to taste

Fry onion and peppers until tender. Stir in salt and pepper. Add tomatoes and simmer gently. Add lobster meat with rum or sherry.
Continue to simmer gently for about 10 minutes. Serve with plain boiled rice.

CREAMED CONCH AND CRACKERS

4 conchs
3 hard boiled eggs, diced
1 tablespoon lemon juice
½ cup mayonnaise
1 teaspoon prepared mustard

pepper to taste
1 sweet pepper, finely chopped
2 medium size onions, finely diced
salt to taste

Beat conch, wash properly and boil without salt. Remove conch from water and dice. Add onions, eggs, sweet pepper and lemon juice. Mix in mayonnaise and mustard. Season with salt and pepper to taste. Serve with crackers.

CRACKED CONCH

Prepare conch for cooking in usual way, removing all red parts. Beat thoroughly with steak tenderizer until sinews are shredded. Beat egg and dip conch into egg. Roll in cracker meal. Fry until golden. Serve with lime, hot sauce and chips. One large conch yields one serving.
(cracker meal) crushed crackers like bread crumbs.

CRAWFISH THERMIDOR

1 average crawfish with shell
2 tablespoons butter/margarine
   salt and pepper to taste
2 shallots, chopped
2–3 mushrooms, chopped

1/3 white sauce
1 teaspoon parsley, chopped
1 cup white sauce
Parmesan cheese, grated

Split the crawfish lengthwise, clean and dot with 1 tablespoon of butter or margarine. Season with salt and pepper. Broil for 18 to 20 minutes. Melt 1 tablespoon butter or margarine in a saucepan; add shallots, mushrooms and wine. Cook until reduced to 1/3 the original quantity. Add parsley, mustard and white sauce. Cook just to combine the ingredients, stirring with a whip, without boiling. Remove the crawfish from shell (save shell) and dice, and mix with 2/3 of the sauce. Put a little of the sauce into the shell, add the crawfish mixture, and spread with the remaining sauce. Sprinkle parmesan cheese and brown under a hot broiler.

WHITE SAUCE

2 tablespoons butter/margarine
1 – 1½ to 2 tablespoons flour
1 cup milk

¼ teaspoon salt
dash of pepper
2 egg yolks – if desired

Melt butter or margarine in a saucepan over low heat. Add and blend in flour, stirring with a whip. Gradually add milk stirring constantly; add seasonings. Remove from heat and stir in egg yolks.

SHRIMP WITH PINEAPPLE

24 large shrimp, cleaned, peeled and cooked
1 tablespoon cornflour
½ pint pineapple juice
2 tablespoons soya sauce
1 tablespoon honey
1 tablespoon vinegar
¼ teaspoon ginger powder
1 small tin of pineapple chunks

Blend cornflour with a little of the pineapple juice. Combine with remaining juice, soya sauce, honey, vinegar and ginger. Cook over a low heat, stirring until thickened.
Thread shrimps and pineapple chunks alternately on to skewers and dip into sauce. Grill until slightly golden in colour.

CURRIED LOBSTER

Lobster meat
4 tablespoons curry powder
1 large ripe tomato, chopped
pepper to taste
6 tablespoons butter
1 large onion, sliced
salt to taste
1 cup meat stock or water

Pour cooking oil into frying pan. Add onion and saute until soft. Add curry powder and cook about 5 minutes. Add tomato and continue cooking for a few minutes. Add lobster, seasonings and stock or water. Simmer for 30 minutes. Serve with boiled rice.

CRAWFISH AND RICE

3 medium crawfish (uncooked)
2 tablespoons oil
½ small onion, chopped
1/8 teaspoon thyme
2 tbsp. tomato paste
3 cups water
¼ teaspoon pepper
1 teaspoon salt

Heat oil in saucepan and saute crawfish, onion and thyme for five minutes. Stir in tomato paste and water; bring to boil. Add rice, salt, and pepper and cook covered for 1 hour, or until liquid is absorbed and rice is tender.

PAN FRIED GROUPER FINGERS

Grouper fillets cut into finger size
Beer
Flour
Salt and pepper

Marinate grouper pieces in beer for one hour. Dry fish well, pressing between absorbent paper. Roll in seasoned flour and shake off excess flour. Fry in hot oil to a depth of 1/8 inch. Fry quickly, turning once. Allow approximately ten minutes cooking time, depending on thickness of the slices. Drain on absorbent paper. Serve with tartar sauce and or lemon slices.

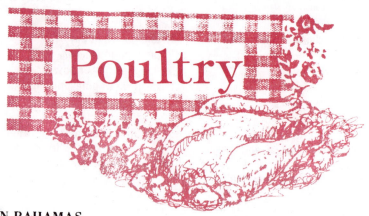

Poultry

CHICKEN BAHAMAS

1 3 lb. chicken
2 cups cooked rice or spaghetti
3 ozs. cashew nuts

* hot pepper sauce to taste
* salt
2 chopped onions

Boil a chicken in the usual way. Reserve stock. Cut chicken into pieces and arrange on a bed of rice, or spaghetti. Prepare a sauce by pounding cashew nuts with some hot pepper sauce and a pinch of salt.

Fry two onions and add to nut mixture, with some of the chicken stock. Pour over the chicken.

CHICKEN AND RICE

1 chicken, cut into serving portions
    salt and pepper
1½ cups rice, uncooked

2 cans (10½ oz) cream of mushroom soup
5 cups water

Salt and pepper chicken and place in large baking dish or casserole. Mix soup with water. Place rice in baking dish over chicken. Pour soup mixture over chicken and rice. Cover and bake at 350 degrees F for one hour or until rice and chicken are tender.

CHICKEN SOUSE

1 4lb. stewing chicken
1 stalk celery, cut up
1 medium onion, sliced thin
1 small sweet pepper, cut into
    thin strips

1 teaspoon salt
4 oz noodles, uncooked
    water

Cut chicken into serving portions; cover with cold water; add celery, onion, sweet pepper and salt; heat to boiling. Reduce heat and simmer for 1 hour or until chicken is almost done; add noodles and simmer 5 minutes longer. Add more water if needed to retain cream soup consistency.

TROPICAL CHICKEN

4 young coconuts	1 diced onion
1 small chicken	½ cup corn kernels
2 cups chicken broth	3 tablespoons curry powder
1 cup rice	* salt, pepper
1 cup chopped pineapple	

Slice off top of coconuts and take a thin slice off the bottoms also, so that the coconut will stand upright. Pour off water and reserve.

Steam chicken in coconut water. When tender, remove, cool and shred the meat. Steam rice in 2 cups of broth (adding water if needed). Mix in pineapple, onions, corn and curry powder. Add seasoning.

Stuff coconuts with this mixture, placing alternate layers with the shredded chicken. Replace tops on coconut and sit in a shallow pan of water. Bake in a moderate oven for one hour. If water in pan evaporates add more.

SUNDAY CHICKEN

3 large chicken breasts, halved	¼ cup chopped green pepper
flour	1 cup chicken broth, stock or water
salt and pepper	1 can condensed cream of chicken soup
¼ cup butter/margarine	¼ cup white wine
1 can (3oz) sliced mushrooms	¼ teaspoon thyme

Wash chicken and dry well. Roll in flour seasoned with salt and pepper. Place in skillet with butter or margarine and brown slowly. Arrange browned chicken, skin side up, in casserole. Add mushrooms and green peppers to drippings in skillet and cook until tender, stirring frequently. Add broth, stock or water and soup, stirring until smooth Add wine and thyme; season. Heat to boiling. Pour sauce over chicken. Cover and bake in moderate moderate oven (350°F) for 25 minutes. Uncover; continue baking 25 to 35 minutes or until chickn is tender. Serve with rice or thin noodles.

A DIFFERENT STUFFING FOR ROASTED CHICKEN

1 cup cooked rice	3 diced cooked chicken livers
½ cup raisins	2 ozs. butter
¼ cup finely chopped onions	1 egg
* chopped parsley	

Mash the chicken livers and mix all ingredients together, working the butter well into mixture. Add the beaten egg last to bind.

CHICKEN MARINATED IN ORANGE

3 chicken breasts, split in half
½ cup orange juice
1 teaspoon salt
½ teaspoon pepper
½ teaspoon ground marjoram
½ teaspoon basil
½ teaspoon garlic salt

Remove skin from chicken, wash chicken and wipe dry. Combine remaining ingredients. Place chicken in baking dish or casserole. Pour orange juice over chicken,, and refrigerate at least 1 hour. Bake uncovered, in a pre-heated oven at 350 degrees F. for about 60 minutes, basting occasionally.

PIGEONS WITH CABBAGE

2 pigeons
1 small cabbage
1 onion
2 pieces bacon
½ cup water
* juice of 1 lime
½ cup raisins
* a pinch of salt
* sugar and pepper to taste

Cut the birds in half down the backbone. Melt fat from bacon and fry the birds in this. Remove birds.

Slice onion and saute in the same pan. Add sugar and raisins. Shred cabbage and add to the pan. Stir to coat.

Heat water and lime juice and add to pan with a sprinkle of salt.

Place the pieces of pigeons on top of the cabbage. Cover and simmer for about 1 hour. Season to taste.

PIGEON PIE

3 pigeons cut into pieces
* salt and pepper
3 tablespoons oil
* diced ham
2 cups chicken broth

Season pigeons with salt and pepper and fry in oil. Add diced ham and stock. Place in a deep pie dish and cover with crust. Bake in 350° oven 30 minutes or till crust is lightly browned.

PIE CRUST

1 cup flour
4 ozs. butter, margarine or shortening
2-3 tablespoons cold water
* pinch of salt

Sift together flour and salt. Mix fat into flour by using 2 knives and "cutting" in the fat till it is pea-sized and coated with flour. Sprinkle water over flour using a minimum amount to moisten mixture. Shape mixture into a mound and roll out. Cut to fit dish.

ROAST PIGEON WITH RICE STUFFING

- 4 pigeons, dressed
- 8 slices bacon, diced
- ½ cup celery, chopped
- 1 onion chopped
- 2 cups rice, uncooked
- 4 cups chicken stock or broth
- 4 eggs beaten
- salt and pepper to taste

Place bacon in skillet and fry until crisp. Remove bacon and brown celery and onion in drippings. Boil rice in chicken stock until tender; add bacon, celery, onion and eggs. Season with salt and peper. Stuff pigeons with the rice stuffing and place on mounds of remaining rice. Bake in moderate oven (350 degrees F) for one hour and 15 minutes.

PIGEONS WITH PINEAPPLE

- ½ of a ripe pineapple
- 4 squabs (young pigeons)
- ¼ cup butter
- ¼ cup paté
- 4 tablespoons brandy or rum if preferred
- * salt, pepper to taste
- ½ cup pineapple juice

Peel, slice and dice pineapple. Wash and dry squabs. Into each body cavity put 1 tablespoon pate and a piece of pineapple. Close cavity and rub squabs with salt and pepper.

Melt ½ of the butter in a heavy casserole and brown the squabs. Do not prick the skins.

Flame with 1 tablespoon brandy or rum (heat, ignite and pour over squabs). Pour in the remaining butter, and roast squabs in 350° oven uncovered, basting often, for about 45 minutes.

While squabs are roasting, poach slices of pineapple in the rest of liquor for 10 minutes. Arrange slices on the squabs to serve.

BRAISED DUCKLING

- 1   3½–4 lb. duckling
- 4 ozs. butter
- 2 onions
- 2 carrots
- ¼ cup brandy or wine
- 1 cup chicken stock
- ½ lb. young sliced turnips
- 2 ozs. butter
- * salt, pepper to taste

Brown duck on all sides in a casserole. Put in the onions and sliced carrots, browning them also.

Pour in the liquor and all the stock with salt and pepper. Place in a moderate oven 350° and baste frequently.

When duck is ready, keep it warm. Strain the liquid, remove vegetables and reduce the sauce.

Serve with the young turnips which have been cooked whilst duck was braising. Blanch the turnips first, then saute in butter.

WHITE CROWN PIGEON OR ANY OTHER DOVE WITH CREAM

4 **Crown pigeons**
4 slices bacon
4 tablespoons butter

¼ pint cream (or evaporated milk)
* a few black olives
* salt and pepper to taste

Cover the breast of each bird with a slice of bacon and season. Place 1 tablespoon butter inside each bird.

Roast in a hot 400-450° oven for 30 minutes. Remove birds, drain off surplus fat and add cream to the pan.

Simmer slowly and season to taste. Add olives, and pour over the birds.

SALMI OF DUCK

1 duck
2 ozs. butter
1 oz. flour
1 onion, chopped

1½ pints chicken stock (chicken cubes melted in water)
* salt, pepper
* brandy or wine

Roast duck, cook till slightly underdone. Cut into neat joints.

Melt 1 oz. butter and fry onion. Add stock, simmer for 1 hour and strain. Melt remaining butter, stir in flour and add the stock. Season and simmer 15 minutes.

Add the pieces of duck and cook 20 minutes longer. Brandy or wine is usually added to taste.

DUCK AND PINEAPPLE

1 4lb. duck
1 tin pineapple slices
2 tablespoons oil
2 tablespoons soya sauce

1 tablespoon rum
½ cup water
2 tablespoons brown sugar
* a pinch of salt

Clean and roast the duck. Cool, remove bones and slice. Drain pineapple slices and dice.

Place duck and pineapple in alternate layers in a casserole. Add the pineapple juice mixed with oil, soya sauce, rum, water, sugar and salt.

Bake in moderate oven for 1 hour. Serve with rice and green salad.

NASSAU CHICKEN

1 chicken
  cut into serving portions
1 cup evaporated milk
1 can (10½ oz) cream of mushroom soup

chopped parsley
paprika
garlic salt

Spread out chicken in one layer in a casserole or shallow baking pan. Sprinkle with garlic salt. Mix soup with the evaporated milk and pour over the chicken. Sprinkle the chopped parsley and paprika on top. Bake uncovered at 350°F for 1½ hours.

CHICKEN CASSEROLE

¼ lb. chicken
¼ cup milk
¼ cup flour
1 teaspoon salt
2 cups evaporated milk or cream

3/4 cup fat
1 can mushrooms, stems and pieces
1½ tablespoons chopped onion
¼ teaspoon pepper

Cut chicken into serving portions; dip into milk then into mixture of flour and pepper. Brown chicken in fat and place in deep baking dish. Saute mushrooms in fat remaining in pan or skillet 5 minutes; add with onion to chicken. Cover with the evaporated milk or cream. **Bake** in moderate oven (350 degrees F.) until chicken is tender and the liquid cooks to **a** thick sauce or about 1½ hours.

Meats

BEEF CURRY WITH GREEN BANANAS

- 3 peeled green bananas cut in ¼" slices
- 1½ lbs. stewing beef
- 3 tablespoons oil
- 2 tablespoons curry powder
- 2 onions
- 1½ tablespoons flour
- ½ cup tomato ketchup
- ½ teaspoon salt
- ½ cup rum

Boil bananas in salted water for 20 minutes. Drain and reserve.
Cut beef into cubes and brown in oil. Transfer to a saucepan.
Add sliced onions. Stir in flour, salt and tomato ketchup and cook for 5 minutes. Cover with curry powder mixed in some water. Stir and simmer for 1½ hrs. Add rum and green banana slices. Heat through.

BEEF AND MANGO IN BEER

- 12 ozs. minced beef
- 1 cup Kalik Beer
- 1 cup water
- ½ cup mango chutney
- * pinch of salt and onion powder
- 1 dessertspoon soya sauce
- ½ cup rice
- 1 cup green peas

Combine first six ingredients in a casserole and bake in oven for 1 hour at 350°. Add rice and cook for ½ hour. Just before serving add the peas.

SALTED BEEF AND BANANA CASSEROLE

- ¼ lb. diced, cooked, salted beef
- 2 eggs
- 1 cup grated cheese
- ½ cup milk
- 1 cup diced ripe bananas
- * salt, pepper, marjoram

Beat eggs, stir in cheese, beef, milk, pepper, marjoram and bananas. Use very little salt, if any. Turn into a casserole and bake for about 40 minutes in a 350° oven.

SOUSE

2 lbs tripe
2 lbs chitterlings
2 lbs. pigs feet, cleaned
   bird peppers to taste
1 cup old sour or lime juice to taste

1 teaspoon pickling spice
1 bay leaf
1 medium onion, sliced
   salt to taste

Cook cleaned tripe, chitterlings and cut up pigs feet, in water to cover. Boil 10 minutes and discard water. Add fresh water to cover, pickling spice, bay leaf, onion, peppers and salt; simmer until tender, about 1 hour. Add old sour or lime juice.

BANANA MEAT ROLLS

1½ small onion, chopped
1 celery heart, chopped
1 tablespoon butter/margarine
   cream sauce

1 cup cooked ground meat
2 bananas, sliced
   biscuit dough (see menu below)
   parsley, chopped

Saute onion and celery in butter or margarine and combine with cold meat and sliced bananas. Roll biscuit dough thin and spread meat mixture over it. Roll dough jelly-roll fashion and slice pieces off the completed roll. Place in a greased pan and bake at 375–400 degrees F. until browned. Serve with cream and garnish with chopped parsley.

BISCUIT DOUGH

2 cups sifted flour
3 teaspoons baking powder
½ to ¾ cup milk

½ teaspoon salt
¼ cup shortening

Cut shortening into sifted dry ingredients until like coarse crumbs, and make a well; add milk. Stir quickly and lightly with a fork only until dough follows fork around bowl. Turn out dough on lightly floured board. Dough should be soft. Knead gently 10 to 12 strokes. Roll as directed above. Any left over dough can be made into biscuits and bake on ungreased baking sheet in very hot oven (450 degrees F.) 12 to 15 minutes.

RUMP STEAK CASSEROLE

2 lbs. steak
¼ lb. butter
1 dessertspoon sugar
1 cup vinegar
1 cup beef stock (tin of beef bouillon or consomme)

* salt, pepper, nutmeg and ginger to taste
1 teaspoon marjoram
* chopped tomatoes, optional

Cut steaks into cubes and marinate for 2 hours in sugar, vinegar, seasoning and herbs. Melt butter and brown beef cubes. Moisten with some of the marinade.

Place meat in a casserole with 1 cup of beef stock. Cover and bake in a 350° oven until tender.

Skim off fat and add a few chopped tomatoes if desired.

BAKED PORK CHOPS

6 pork chops
½ cup flour, seasoned with salt, pepper and paprika
2 tablespoons shortening

6 lemon slices
2/3 cup catsup
2/3 cup water
3 tablespoons brown sugar

Place pork chops in seasoned flour. Place shortening in skillet and heat; brown pork chops in hot fat turning to brown on both sides. Place in one layer in shallow baking dish and top each chop with a lemon slice. Combine catsup, water and brown sugar and pour over the chops. Cover and bake in pre-heated oven at 350°F for thirty minutes. Uncover and bake 20-30 minutes longer. Add water if desired.

MUTTON STEW

3 lbs. goat meat
1 teaspoon hot sauce
1 cup chopped onions
* oil, salt, flour
1 cup sliced carrots

1 cup chopped tomatoes
1 cup sliced potatoes
4 cups hot water
* some small flour dumplings

Dredge cubed meat with flour and salt and brown in hot oil. Add water and simmer until meat is tender.

Add sauce, onions, and vegetables. Cook until vegetables are ready. This process should take about 2 hours.

When all is ready add the dumplings which will cook very quickly. Add more liquid if necessary.

STEAMED ABACO WILD HOG

2 lbs. wild hog meat
   cut into 2-inch cubes
   bones included
Salt, pepper and cayenne pepper

Frying fat such as bacon drippings
1 large onion, sliced
1 to 2 tablespoons tomato paste

Place meat and salt in cooking pot and add water to cover; cook until tender 1–1½ hours. Discard water, and brown meat in the pot using bacon fat or any fat preferred; turn meat to brown on all sides. In Dutch oven, saute the onion, using one to two tablespoons fat or oil; add 1-2 tablespoons tomato paste. Stir until heated through and well mixed. Add meat, seasoning and about one cup water. Simmer until sauce thickens.

LIVER WITH SWEET PEPPERS

1 lb. liver sliced thin
4 sweet peppers
1 teaspoon lime juice

1 tablespoon rum
½ cup oil
* salt, pepper, a little flour

Prepare sweet peppers by coring and removing seeds. Wash and cut into strips.
Season liver with salt, pepper and lime juice. Dust with flour and saute quickly in hot oil. Pour the rum over liver. Add the slices of pepper and cook gently for 15-20 minutes.

PORK CHOPS WITH GINGER ALE

4 chops
* fat, salt, pepper

* parsley
* ginger ale

Brown chops lightly in fat. Add seasoning. Place in individual squares of foil. Sprinkle liberally with ginger ale. Fold squares tightly. Place in a baking dish and bake in a 350° oven for about 1½ hours.

PORK CHOPS WITH PINEAPPLE

4 chops
1 cup pineapple chunks
8 prunes or 1 cup raisins
1 teaspoon grated lime peel
* sprinkle of sugar and salt
* breadcrumbs

* a lump of butter
2 cups shredded cabbage
* salt
¼ cup vinegar
1 tablespoon water

Brown chops and sprinkle with salt. In a casserole, place the chops in layers with the pineapple, prunes, peel and sugar.
Cover with breadcrumbs and dot with butter. Bake in a slow oven 300° for 1½ hours.
Serve with shredded cabbage which has been sprinkled with salt and boiled in vinegar and water. When tender, strain and serve hot.

BEEF AND RICE CASSEROLE

1 can whole kernel corn
1 cup rice, uncooked
1 can (8 oz) tomato paste
½ cup water
1 onion, chopped
salt and pepper to taste
1½ lbs. ground beef

Mix together corn, rice, ¾ can of tomato paste, water, onion, salt and pepper; spread in bottom of greased casserole. Season ground beef with salt and pepper and form into 6 patties. Place patties on top of mixture in casserole and cover with topping. Cover casserole and bake at 359 degrees F. for 1 hour.

TOPPING

Remaining ¼ can tomato paste
2 tablespoons catsup
¼ cup water

Mix together.

SPICED BAHAMIAN SOUSE

3 sheep tongue
3 lbs. pig feet
½ lb. tripe
¼ teaspoon spice seed
4 spice leaves
water
1 lb. native mutton
1 lb. native fresh pork
1 pig ear
1 large onion, sliced
hot pepper
salt to taste

Scald all meats for 5 minutes then pour off water. Cut meats into bite size peices. Rinse meats and add enough water to cover. Add onion, spice seed and spice leaves. Season to taste with salt, hot pepper and lime juice. Boil until done in pressure cooker for ¾ hour. Serves 6.

BRAWN (made also with Rabbit using the whole animal)

1 pig's head
* water, pimento leaves
* few cloves
* lime to taste
* salt to taste

Scrape and clean the head and wash with lime juice. Cover with water, pimento leaves, salt and cloves. Boil until tender.

Cut into chunks discarding the bones. Add lime juice to the liquid and pour over the brawn in a casserole. Place in the refrigerator to congeal.

NASSAU CHOP SUEY

1 lb. beef and/or pork	1 cup onion, thinly sliced
2 tablespoons shortening	¼ cup soy sauce
1 cup water	1 can sliced mushrooms, undrained
½ teaspoon salt	3 tablespoons cornstarch
pepper to taste	1 can bean sprouts, drained
1 cup celery, sliced	4 cups cooked rice

Cut beef and/or pork into ½ inch pieces. Slowly brown the meat in hot shortening; add water, salt and pepper. Cover with tight fitting cover; cook 10 minutes. Add celery and onion, cook 2 minutes. Add mushrooms with liquid. Mix together soy sauce and slowly stir into hot mixture. Cook and stir until thick and bubbly. Add bean sprouts. Serve over hot rice.

MARINATED PORK CHOPS

4 chops	* lime juice
* salt, pepper	* garlic powder

Sprinkle the chops with seasonings and lime juice and marinate for 2 hours. Grill the chops and serve with a green salad. Instead of a dressing pour the juices from the grilling pan.

Vegetables

BEANS IN SOUR CREAM SAUCE

1 lb. green beans (string beans) * salt
2 tablespoons butter

Boil beans uncovered, strain, melt butter, add beans and toss. Season with salt and pepper. Top with this sauce.

SAUCE

1 cup sour cream * a few drops of lime juice
¼ cup milk * a pinch of garlic powder

Mix ingredients together and pour over beans.

BROAD BEAN CUTLETS

1 lb. broad beans (or sugar beans) 1 teaspoon chopped parsley
1 oz. butter 6 ozs. crushed potatoes
2 eggs * bread crumbs
1 teaspoon minced onion * salt and pepper to taste

Cook beans in boiling water with salt and onions. Puree by rubbing through a sieve.
Add melted butter, crushed potatoes, seasoning, and enough of the beaten eggs to bind into a paste. Add enough bread crumbs to shape into cutlets and coat with egg and more bread crumbs. Fry in deep hot fat. Drain and serve warm.

STUFFED BREADFRUIT

medium size breadfruit	1 small chopped onion
tablespoon butter	* a pinch of salt
¼ cup milk	

Stuffed breadfruit is first roasted for an hour in the skin — roasted over charcoal is of course the best way, but it can be done over a gas burner.

When cooked, cut a circle in the top, scoop out heart and discard, then scoop out the flesh.

Crush this, cream with milk and butter and season with a little salt and onion. To this may be added minced beef, codfish and ackee, or left over stew etc.

Pack into the cavity, wrap with foil and put into the oven to warm through before serving.

BAKED CABBAGE

cups shredded cabbage	1 teaspoon salt
cups breadcrumbs	1 teaspoon prepared mustard
cup grated cheese	2 cups milk
eggs	1/8 teaspoon pepper

Cover cabbage with water, bring to a boil and drain. In a shallow 2 qrt. dish, arrange cabbage, breadcrumbs and cheese in layers.

Beat eggs with salt, pepper and mustard. Add milk and pour over the cabbage. Let stand for 15 minutes. Bake for 45 minutes in a 350° oven.

FRUITED CABBAGE

½ lbs. shredded cabbage	1 cup water
ozs. raisins	1 cup diced pineapple
diced onions	* juice of 1 lime

Mix cabbage with fruit and onions. Add 1 cup water, lime juice and a pinch of salt. Cook for about 40 minutes or until liquid has evaporated.

CALLALOO BAKE

bunch callaloo cooked and diced	2 tablespoons grated cheese
diced onion	¼ cup crushed potatoes
slices bacon fried and diced	1 cup breadcrumbs

Mix first three ingredients in a casserole. Top with breadcrumbs, cheese and potatoes. Bake for about 35 minutes in a moderate oven.

FRUITY CALLALOO

1 bunch callaloo, chopped * salt, pepper
1 cup grapefruit juice

    Wash and prepare callaloo, add salt and pepper. Put into a pot with grapefruit juice. Cook quickly for 10 minutes. Drain, season and serve.

CARROT AMBROSIA

12 carrots 2 tablespoons sugar
2 tablespoons butter or margarine 2 sliced oranges

    Glaze 12 small carrots by melting the sugar and butter in a pan and turning the carrots either sliced or whole, in the mixture over a moderate heat till golden brown.
    Add 2 sliced oranges and reheat to serve.

MINT GLAZED CARROTS

12 small carrots (pre-cooked) 1 teaspoon mint sauce
¼ cup butter ¼ cup sugar

    Simmer carrots in the butter. Add mint sauce and sugar. Cook until sugar has melted.

CAULIFLOWER CUSTARD

1 cauliflower 1 cup milk
2 eggs * salt, nutmeg, garlic powder

    Boil cauliflower in some salt and water. When cool, break off flowerets and put into greased dish.
    Beat 2 eggs with milk and garlic powder. Pour over cauliflower. Sprinkle with nutmeg. Bake until set.

CHO CHOS BAKED WITH CHEESE

3 cho chos, boiled and sliced * dabs of butter or margarine
½ cup grated cheese

    Place chocho slices in a casserole, in alternate layers with grated cheese and dabs of butter, ending with cheese. Bake until cheese has melted and is crisp on top.

OKRA AND RICE

1–2 tablespoons vegetable oil
8–12 fresh okra cut into small pieces
1 cup rice
1 tablespoon tomato paste

1 teaspoon thyme
salt to taste
2 cups water

Saute okra in hot oil, stirring until slightly softened. Add tomato paste, thyme and salt; cook and stir a minute or so. Blend in rice and water. Bring to a vigorous boil. Turn down heat as low as possible; cover saucepan and leave over low heat for 14 minutes. Turn off heat, but without removing lid, allow rice to steam for an additional 10 minutes. Never stir rice; keep lid on until served.

RICE AND PUMPKIN

1 tablespoon shortening or oil
1 small onion, chopped
1 small sweet pepper, cut up
salt and pepper to taste

3 tablespoons tomato paste
¼ medium size pumpkin peeled
2 cups long grain, rice, uncooked

Place oil in cooking pot over medium heat. Add onion and sweet pepper and cook to soften, stirring constantly. Add tomato paste and stir to blend; add cubed pumpkin and 4 cups water. Season to taste. Add rice and cook at low heat until water is absorbed and rice tender. Correct seasoning. Add more water if needed.

BEETS WITH ORANGE SAUCE

6 beets (about 1½ lbs.)
2 tablespoons sugar
1 tablespoon cornstarch
¼ teaspoon salt

¼ cup orange juice
1 tablespoon lime juice
½ teaspoonful grated orange rind
1 tablespoon butter

Boil beets in salted water until tender Drain, reserving the water. Peel the beets and dice.
Combine sugar cornstarch and salt in the top of a double boiler. Gently stir in ¼ cup of liquid from the cooked beets and the orange juice. Cook over boiling water until thick and smooth, stirring constantly.
Remove from the heat. Stir in remaining ingredients. Add the diced beets and mix lightly. Keep warm over hot water until ready to serve.

PEAS AND RICE

- 2 tablespoons cooking oil
- 1 small onion, sliced
- ½ green pepper, sliced
- 1½ tablespoons salt
- 3 cups water
- ¾ cups cooked pigeon peas
- ½ cup tomato paste
- ¼ lb. salt pork; diced
- 1 stalk celery, chopped
- pepper to taste
- 2 cups uncooked rice
- 2 teaspoons thyme

Fry pork in frying pan. Add cooking oil. Saute the onion until wilted. Add sweet pepper, celery, thyme and tomato paste, allow to simmer for 5 minutes. Add pigeon peas and steam for a further 5 minutes. Pour the mixture into a pot. Add water. Season.

CONCH RICE

- 3 conchs
- 1 large onion, sliced
- 2 stalks celery, chopped
- 1 sweet pepper, diced
- pepper to taste
- 2 teaspoons thyme
- 3 ripe tomatoes, chopped
- 3 tablespoons cooking oil
- 2 tablespoons salt
- 5 cups water
- 4 cups uncooked rice

Bruise and clean conch. Boil in unsalted water until tender. Remove conch from water, cut into bite sized pieces and set aside. Saute onion, celery and sweet pepper in cooking oil until soft but not brown. Stir in tomatoes, conch and thyme and simmer for 5 minutes. Add water and season with salt and pepper. Bring to a boil. Add rice and cook over low flame until dry, stirring occasionally.

ANOTHER PEAS AND RICE

- 1 small onion
- ½ teaspoon leaf thyme
- 2 cups uncooked rice
- ½ cup ham fat, cubed
- salt to taste
- ½ small tin tomato paste
- 1 large tin pigeon peas
- 3 cups water
- pepper to taste
- 3 tablespoons cooking oil

Fry out ham fat, remove from pan and save. Add cooking oil. Saute onion until lightly browned. Add thyme and tomato paste and simmer for about 5 minutes. Drain pigeon peas and add to tomato mixture. Pour in water and season to taste. Allow mixture to boil and add to rice. Cook over medium heat for about 20 to 30 minutes or until rice is tender.

PEAS AND GRITS

1 large tin pigeon peas
1 medium size onion, sliced
1 teaspoon thyme
½ sweet pepper, diced
2 tablespoons tomato paste
4 cups water
2½ cups grits
1 teaspoon salt
½ hot pepper
2 tablespoons cooking oil

Pour oil in frying pan. Add onion and sweet pepper and saute lightly. Add tomato paste and allow to steam down for about 5 minutes. Add thyme and hot pepper. Pour the mixture into a pot with peas and water. Allow the mixture to a boil for 10 minutes. Add grits, stirring constantly for about 10 minutes then lower flame and continue cooking for 15 to 20 minutes.

BAHAMIAN MACARONI AND CHEESE

8 ounces elbow macaroni, cooked
1 tablespoon onion, finely chopped
1 tablespoon green pepper
1 can evaporated milk
1 tablespoon celery, finely chopped
6 ounces Cheddar cheese
dash of pepper
salt to taste

Add the onion, green pepper and celery to the macaroni; stir. Add one half of the cheese and stir over low heat until melted. Season and stir in evaporated milk. Spoon into a well greased baking pan and sprinkle remaining cheese evenly over the top. Bake in a preheated oven at 350 degrees F. for 20 minutes. Let stand for 10 minutes and cut into squares to serve.

OKRA WITH TOMATOES

12 boiled okras
4 chopped tomatoes
4 tablespoons breadcrumbs
1 oz. butter
1 oz. flour
½ pt. milk
* salt, pepper, thyme

Melt butter, stir in flour for 2 minutes. Remove from heat and add the milk gradually. Season and cook over low heat for 5 minutes.

Chop okras, mix with tomatoes and 2 tablespoons of the breadcrumbs. Turn into a baking dish and pour flour-milk mixture over this.

Sprinkle with remaining breadcrumbs and bake for about 15 minutes in a moderate oven.

STUFFED PAWPAW (PAPAYA)

1 green pawpaw (just streaked with yellow)	1 sweet pepper
2 onions	1 hot pepper
2 cloves garlic	1 tablespoon breadcrumbs
2 tomatoes	1 egg
2 slices of ham or bacon	* salt

Wash pawpaw. Cut off end and scoop out seeds. Chop onions, garlic, peppers and tomatoes and stew for 20 minutes.

Grill bacon and dice. Mix with breadcrumbs, egg and salt. Add to the vegetable stew and pack into pawpaw.

Cover with foil and set in a pan with a cup of water to bake in a moderate oven for an hour. Skin should not be eaten.

BAKED SWEET POTATO

Allow ½ potato per person	3 tablespoons Red Stripe Beer
3 baked potatoes in skin	2 ozs. butter
2 tablespoons grated coconut	* salt, cinnamon

Cut potatoes in half, scoop out pulp. Crush with beer and butter. Add coconut and salt. Sprinkle with cinnamon and bake through to heat and serve.

PUMPKIN PUFF

2 cups hot mashed pumpkin	1 egg beaten
2 tablespoons butter	2 tablespoons flour
2 tablespoons minced onion	* a tip of baking powder
¼ cup milk	* salt, pepper

Heat oven to 400°. Combine all ingredients and bake in a casserole for 30 minutes

---

YAM CASSEROLE

Yellow yam boiled and sliced	1 cup white sauce
3 hard boiled eggs	* salt, pepper
½ cup grated cheese	

Place slices of yam alternately with sliced eggs and cheese in a casserole. Sprinkle with salt and pepper.

Make a white sauce and moisten yam mixture with 1 cup or more. Bake in a moderate oven till cheese is melted.

Salads

QUICK CONCH SALAD

3   conchs, cut into small cubes
½   cup finely diced sweet pepper
½   cup finely diced cucumber
½   cup lime juice
½   cup finely diced celery
½   cup finely diced onion
2   fresh tomatoes, chopped
    salt to taste

Mix all ingredients together and allow to marinate. Serves 6.

AVOCADO AND GRAPEFRUIT

2   avocados
2   grapefruits
1   dessertspoon oil
1   dessertspoon vinegar
*   salt to taste

Peel and remove seeds from avocados. Slice in circles. Place in individual plates. Fill centres with grapefruit segments. Cover with dressing of oil and vinegar.

BROAD BEAN SALAD

1   lb. broad beans (shelled)
½   lb. potatoes
2   hard boiled eggs
1   tablespoon diced sour pickles
*   salt, pepper, oil and vinegar

Boil the beans in some salted water. Boil potatoes. Mix beans, diced potatoes, chopped eggs and pickles and season to taste. Moisten with oil and vinegar.

THREE-BEAN SALAD

1 cup cooked string beans
1 cup cooked red beans or peas
1 cup cooked broad beans
½ cup vinegar

¼ cup oil
½ onion finely chopped
* chopped mint leaves
* a pinch of sugar and salt

Mix beans together and toss with the last five ingredients.

STRING BEAN SALAD

½ lb. cooked beans
1 dessertspoon oil
1 dessertspoon vinegar

½ chopped onion
* a few peanuts

Boil beans in salted water. Drain and dry in a cloth. Serve with oil and vinegar dressing and some chopped peanuts and onions.

BREADFRUIT SALAD

1 breadfruit
2 hardboiled eggs

* mayonnaise, salt, pepper
* a chopped shallot or small onion

Peel, dice, and boil breadfruit till just firm. Combine with eggs, shallot, salt and pepper. Moisten with mayonnaise.

CALLALOO SALAD

1 lb. callaloo or spinach
6 boiled, sliced potatoes
6 thin slices of cheese

½ cup mayonnaise
* squeeze of lime juice

Plunge callaloo into boiling water for 3 minutes. Drain and chop.
Mix with cold sliced potatoes and thin slices of cheese. Dress with mayonnaise to which is added a squeeze of lime juice.

CARROT AND RAISIN SALAD

6 large carrots
½ cup raisins

* oil and vinegar
* lettuce or cabbage leaves

Shred carrots, mix with raisins and sprinkle with oil and vinegar. Serve on leaves.

CHICKEN SALAD

2 lbs. chicken
2 cups diced pineapple
6 hard boiled eggs
1 cup green peas

½ cup mayonnaise
1 dessertspoon minced parsley
* salt

Boil chicken, remove the meat and chill. When chilled mix with pineapple, peas, salt and parsley, and toss with mayonnaise. Finally, crumble in the yolks and garnish with egg whites.

CHOCHO SALAD

3 chochos, peeled, sliced and boiled
2 sliced onions

* oil and vinegar
* salt and pepper

Place chochos in a shallow dish. Sprinkle with pepper, salt, oil and vinegar. Cover with sliced onions and some more of the oil and vinegar.

BAHAMIAN CONCH SALAD

12 young queen conch
3 hot peppers
½ cup vinegar

¼ cup oil
2 sliced onions
* salt
* lime juice

Cover conch with water and bring to a boil, by which time it should be easy to remove the meat. Wash with lime juice and clean.

Dice and mix with chopped hot peppers, vinegar, oil, sliced onions and salt. This is a popular salad in the Bahamas.

CUCUMBER AND SOUR CREAM SALAD

1 cup sour cream
1 teaspoon vinegar
1 tablespoon chopped mint

* a pinch of sugar
* sliced cucumbers

Mix together sour cream, vinegar, mint and sugar. Pour this over the sliced cucumbers. Marinate for an hour before serving.

CRAWFISH SALAD

2-3 crawfish tails
3 hard cooked eggs, chopped
½ cup celery, finely choppped
¼ teaspoon salt

¼ cup onions, finely chopped
juice of 1 or 2 limes
3 tablespoons mayonnaise
hot pepper

Cut up crawfish into small pieces and marinate in lime juice for ½ hour. Add remaining ingredients and toss lightly. Chill in refrigerator and serve garnished with crisp lettuce and tomato slices.

LOBSTER SALAD

1 cup mayonnaise
1 teaspoon onion powder
* lobster meat
* dressing

1 dessertspoon creole sauce
* shredded lettuce
* a few drops of lime juice

For each person arrange shredded lettuce on a plate. Top with a helping of lobster meat which has been tossed with the dressing. Decorate with olives and strips of celery.

ONION SALAD

12 small onions
2 chopped tomatoes
* a handful of currants or raisins

* salt — parsley
* oil and vinegar to taste

Peel and boil onions in a small amount of salted water. When cooked add tomatoes, oil, vinegar, parsley and currants. Serve cold.

SWEET PEPPER SALAD

2 red sweet peppers
2 green sweet peppers

2 tablespoons oil
* oil and vinegar to taste

Cut and slice peppers. Take out veins and seeds. Saute quickly in oil. Drain. Add oil and vinegar with a pinch of salt.

SHRIMP SALAD WITH COCONUT CREAM

1 cup milk
1 cup grated coconut
1 tablespoon oil
1 teaspoon salt
2 minced shallots

2 chopped sweet peppers
2 tablespoons soya sauce
1 tablespoon chopped peanuts
2 lbs. shrimp (cooked and peeled)

Combine milk and coconut in saucepan and bring to boil. Remove from heat and soak for 30 minutes. Press through a sieve to extract cream. Discard pulp.

Heat oil, and fry the shallots and peppers. Remove from heat. Add soya sauce and peanuts. Combine with coconut cream.

Arrange shrimps on a dish and pour dressing over them. Reserve a few shrimps for decoration and chill slightly to serve.

SALAD CREOLE

2/3 pineapple
1/3 of a tomato per person
½ cup fresh cream
1 tablespoon ketchup

* pinch of salt
* squeeze of lime juice
* chopped onion

Cut pineapple into thin strips and dice tomato. Combine next 4 ingredients and pour over salad. Serve on lettuce leaves and top with a sprinkle of chopped onions.

TROPICAL SALAD

1 cup grated coconut
1 cup diced pineapple

1 cup seeded tangerine segments
1 cup mayonnaise

Combine ingredients and serve on cabbage leaves or lettuce leaves.

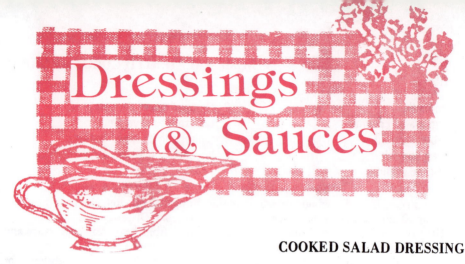

Dressings & Sauces

COOKED SALAD DRESSING

2 ozs. butter	1 teaspoon dry mustard
1 beaten egg	¼ cup vinegar
½ cup milk	* pinch of salt
¼ cup sugar	

Melt butter. Add egg and milk and stir in sugar, salt and mustard, which have been blended with some vinegar.

Gradually add the rest of vinegar. Stir over low heat in a double boiler until thickened. Do not allow to boil. Cool and refrigerate.

HONEY DRESSING FOR FRUIT SALADS

½ cup vinegar	½ cup lime juice
2 tablespoons honey	3 tablespoons crushed pineapple

Mix together and chill.

A BASIC WHITE SAUCE

Melt 2 tablespoons margarine on low heat. Add ½ cup flour slowly, whilst stirring, with 1 cup of milk, and a pinch of salt until this thickens.
Do not allow to burn.

A HOT DRESSING

½ cup peanut butter	¼ cup milk
¼ cup tomato ketchup	* a few drops hot sauce

Mix to a paste adding more milk if needed. Use over onions, cucumbers or sweet peppers.

An elegant table setting for a meal complete with a selected wine of choice.

A delicious main course in Caribbean cuisine is fish, using the flavours of the island.

Prawns is a favourite seafood in Caribbean Cuisine.

Sugary desserts usually complete a Caribbean meal

OIL AND VINEGAR

¼ cup oil
1/6 cup vinegar

1 dessertspoon dry mustard
* pinch of salt

Mix well together.

MY SALAD DRESSING

¼ cup vinegar
2 teaspoons sugar

1 teaspoon mint jelly
* a squeeze of lime and a pinch of salt

Blend together and chill.

A DRESSING FOR SEA FOOD

4 tablespoons mayonnaise
4 tablespoons french dressing
2 tablespoons mango chutney

1 teaspoon lime juice
* a pinch of curry powder
* salt and pepper to taste

Combine and mix all ingredients.

SPICY DRESSING

3 tablespoons vinegar
2 tablespoons sugar

1 tablespoon powdered ginger

Blend together and chill. Delicious on crisp green salad.

---

2 MINUTE MAYONNAISE

1 teaspoon sugar
½ teaspoon salt
¼ teaspoon dry mustard

½ cup evaporated milk
½ cup oil
2 tablespoons vinegar

Mix all ingredients except oil and vinegar. Add oil gradually in a thin stream and beat well. Finally, add vinegar slowly, continuing to beat till smooth.

DEVILS SAUCE

2 tablespoons brown sugar	1 tablespoon guava jelly
1 dessertspoon creole sauce	¼ teaspoon salt
3 tablespoon ketchup	3 tablespoons vinegar
¼ teaspoon hot sauce	

Mix all ingredients together in a saucepan and simmer for 2 minutes. Cool and chill.

EGG SAUCE

½ pt. evaporated milk	1 teaspoon lime juice
2 eggs	½ teaspoon pepper and salt
1 teaspoon vinegar	

Hard boil eggs and chop. Mix with milk and other ingredients. Excellent over salads.

HOT PEPPER SAUCE

4 hot peppers	1 teaspoon ketchup
1 teaspoon oil	1 teaspoon vinegar
1 teaspoon creole sauce	* salt to taste

Put peppers, and other ingredients through a blender or mincer. Bottle. Makes 1 bottle.

MARINA SAUCE

¼ cup oil	3 cups diced tomatoes
1 clove crushed garlic	1 chopped sweet pepper
2 teaspoons minced parsley	* salt to taste

Mix well together and simmer slowly for 30 minutes. Cool and chill.

MARMALADE SAUCE

6 teaspoons dry mustard	2 teaspoons rum
* marmalade to taste	* soya sauce

Mix mustard with some rum to make a paste. Add marmalade and a few drops of soya sauce. Serve with barbecued dishes.

PEANUT SAUCE

2 cups crushed peanuts
1 tablespoon chopped onion
3 tomatoes
1 tablespoon fat
3 cups water
2 teaspoons curry powder
* salt

Put nuts into salted water and boil for 15 minutes. Fry onions and tomatoes and add to peanut mixture with curry powder. Simmer for about 20 minutes, stirring frequently.

PEPPERMINT SAUCE

2 egg whites
2 cups thin cream (evaporated milk)
1 tablespoon sugar
2 tablespoons creme de menthe

Beat egg whites stiff. Fold in cream, sugar and creme de menthe. Good over a fruit salad.

RUM SAUCE

4 ozs. butter
2 ozs. granulated sugar
2 tablespoons rum

Cream butter and sugar and add rum very slowly. Beat well and keep cool.

SABAYON SAUCE

4 ozs. sugar
2 tablespoons sherry
3 egg yolks
* few drops vanilla

Cream sugar and yolks together over a gentle heat. Add vanilla. Gradually add sherry and whisk vigorously until frothy and firm. Use immediately.

SWEET AND SOUR SAUCE

6 chopped shallots
2 tablespoons vinegar
1½ tablespoons brown sugar
½ teaspoon ketchup
1½ cups pineapple juice
1 teaspoon soya sauce
½ cup water
3 teaspoons cornstarch

Mix all ingredients except water and cornstarch and simmer gently for about 40 minutes. Mix cornstarch with water and add to the sauce. Simmer 5 minutes more, stirring until sauce thickens.

Caribbean Chosen Barbecues

BARBECUE COOKING CHART			
RARE	4 - 5 lb. Roast	2 - 2½	hours
MEDIUM	4 - 5 lb. Roast	2½ - 3	hours
WELL DONE	4 - 5 lb. Roast	3 - 4	hours

BACON-WRAPPED FRANKFURTERS

- 1 lb. frankfurters
- 4 ozs. cheddar cheese, sliced
- 8 rashers bacon
- 4 teaspoons mustard

Barbecue the frankfurters over medium coals for about 15 minutes, then slice them lengthways, almost through. Fill with cheese slices and press the frankfurters together again.

Spread the rashers of bacon with mustard and wrap around the frankfurters, securing the ends with wooden cocktail sticks. Place on the grill again and cook over medium coals for a further 5 minutes, or until cheese melts and bacon is crisp. Serve with a mixed green salad and potato chips.

Serves 4.

BAKED RED SNAPPER IN SAVOURY BARBECUE SAUCE

- 1   3 lb. red snapper
- 6 tablespoons butter
- ½ cup chopped onions
- 2 cups chopped celery
- ¼ cup chopped green peppers
- 3 cups canned tomatoes
- 1 tablespoon Worchestershire/ Pickapeppa sauce
- 1 tablespoon ketchup
- 1 teaspoon chili powder
- ½ lemon, finely sliced
- 1 teaspoon salt
- 2 bay leaves
- 2 teaspoons sugar
- 1 red pepper

Preheat oven to 350oF. Dredge snapper inside and out with seasoned flour. Place in baking pan. In a pot, melt butter. Add onions, celery and green peppers. Simmer until celery is tender. Add other remaining ingredients and simmer 15 minutes. Pour sauce over the fish. Bake approximately 45 minutes, basting frequently.

Serves 4—5 people.

BARBECUED CHICKEN

1 2½ lb. chicken, cut in serving pieces	* salt to taste
* black pepper	* garlic

SAUCE

¼ cup chopped onions	¼ teaspoon paprika
½ cup water	½ teaspoon salt
2 tablespoons vinegar	1 teaspoon black pepper
1 tablespoon Worcestershire/ Pickapeppa sauce	1 teaspoon prepared mustard
¼ cup lemon juice	1 teaspoon ketchup
2 tablespoons sugar	1 tablespoon butter
1 cup chili/tomato sauce	* hot pepper sauce to taste

Season chicken liberally with salt, black pepper, garlic. Let stand 1 hour.

To prepare sauce: Saute onions till brown. Add other sauce ingredients and simmer 15 minutes, then cool. Broil chicken. Add sauce when chicken is nearly done (after about 1 hour), basting continually. Serves 4.

BARBECUED CHICKEN WINGS

2 lbs. chicken wings	1 large clove garlic, crushed
3 tablespoons honey	1 stock cube
3 tablespoons vinegar	¼ pint hot water
2 tablespoons sugar	1 tablespoon sherry
3 tablespoons soy sauce	

Cut and trim chicken wings. Place in a bowl. Blend together honey, vinegar, sugar, soy sauce and garlic, and pour over the meat. Dissolve stock cube in the hot water, then add the sherry. Add to the other ingredients in the bowl and stir together. Leave to marinate for 8 to 12 hours or overnight in the refrigerator. Preheat the oven to moderately slow at 335°F. Arrange chicken wings on a rack in a roast pan and baste well with the marinade. Bake, uncovered, until golden brown, basting occasionally with the sauce, turning once during the cooking time.

If served as a party-time snack, eat with fingers and provide a finger bowl of warm water and serviettes to wipe fingers.

BARBECUED CHICKEN WITH SPECIAL SAUCE

1   3 lb. chicken
1   cup tomato sauce or ketchup
1   teaspoon creole sauce
2   tablespoon vinegar

1   teaspoon dry mustard
1   teaspoon sugar
*   a drop or two of hot sauce

Cut chicken into pieces. Season with salt and pepper and grill over hot coals basting frequently with sauce made by combining last 6 ingredients and bring to a boil.

BARBECUED LAMB CHOPS

4   lbs. lamb chops
1   teaspoon prepared mustard
1   piece ginger, beaten
2   medium-sized onions, sliced
1   tablespoon salad oil
1   cup water
*   salt to taste

2   tablespoons chili/tomato sauce
1   tablespoon Worchestershire/
    Pickapeppa sauce
1   tablespoon vinegar
*   hot pepper sauce to taste
*   black pepper

Season chops with mustard, ginger, salt and pepper. Place sliced onions over chops in baking pan. Combine other ingredients and pour over onions and chops. Bake, covered, in moderate oven, basting frequently, for approximately 15-20 minutes or until done. Remove lid 10 minutes before chops are cooked.
Serves 6.

JIFFY BARBECUE SAUCE

½   cup tomato ketchup
1   teaspoon dry mustard
1   teaspoon hot pepper sauce
2   teaspoons mango chutney

2   teaspoons Pickapeppa Sauce
*   liquid from the can of corn & water
    to make ¾ cup

Combine all ingredients and pour over pork chops.

BARBECUED MEAT BALLS

- 1 lb. ground beef
- 2 tablespoons chopped parsley
- 1 tablespoon bread crumbs
- 1 teaspoon salt
- ½ large onion
- 1 sprig thyme, chopped

SAUCE
- 1 large sweet pepper
- 1 clove garlic
- 1 cup ketchup
- 1 teaspoon vinegar
- 1 piece ginger

- 1 egg yolk
- 1 tablespoon soft butter
- 1 teaspoon lemon juice
- 1 teaspoon black pepper
- 1 small sweet pepper
- 2 whole pimento grains

- 1 large onion
- 1 carrot (cut up in long strips)
- 2 tablespoons sugar
- ½ teaspoon salt (to taste)

To prepare sauce: saute sweet pepper, onion, garlic, carrot in butter. Add other ingredients, then simmer for 20 minutes. Meanwhile, combine meatball ingredients, mold into balls. Skewer balls and place over flame, turning and basting continually with sauce. Serves 4.

BARBECUED ORIENTAL CHICKEN

- 1 cup soy sauce
- 1 cup sake (Japanese rice wine) or 1 cup grapefruit juice or 1 cup dry sherry
- ¼ cup cooking oil

- 1 teaspoon sugar
- ½ teaspoon grated fresh ginger root, or ground ginger
- * one 2½ pound chicken, cut up

Mix together soy sauce, sake or grapefruit juice or sherry, sugar and ginger in a large shallow dish. Add chicken, turning to coat both sides. Cover and marinate in refrigerator, several hours or overnight, turning occasionally. Remove chicken from marinade and brush with oil. Grill about 6 inches from source of heat, brushing with marinade and turning frequently until brown and tender.
Serves 4.

BARBECUED PERCH

- 5 lb. perch
- 1 cup celery
- 1 cup onions
- 1 cup ketchup
- 1 tablespoon prepared mustard

- 1 tablespoon Worchestershire/Pickapeppa sauce
- 2 tablespoons vinegar
- 2 tablespoons sugar

Grill fish for 10 minutes. Meanwhile, saute celery and onions. Combine other ingredients, bring to a boil. Baste fish with sauce, cooking for another 10 minutes.
Serves 6-8.

BARBECUED SPARERIBS (BAKED)

Use the American style pork spareribs for this succulent recipe. If you can do the ribs over a good bed of charcoal, attending carefully to the basting, so much the better!

5 to 6 lb. spareribs cut in serving pieces
1 lemon thinly sliced
¼ cup molasses
¼ cup prepared mustard
2 tablespoons vinegar
* salt to taste
2 tablespoons lemon juice
1 teaspoon chili powder
1 tablespoon celery seed
2 tablespoons Pickapeppa sauce
½ cup tomato ketchup

Place spareribs, meat side up, in a shallow pan. Sprinkle with salt. Top with lemon slices.
Bake in a moderate oven 350°F for 30 minutes.
Combine remaining ingredients and blend well. Remove lemon slices. Brush spareribs with mixture; turn and continue baking one hour longer, basting frequently.
Serve hot.

BARBECUED SPARE RIBS

2 lbs. spare ribs, cut in serving pieces
2 teaspoons salt
4 pimento grains, crushed
* oregano
   SAUCE
¼ cup chopped onions
1 tablespoon fat
½ cup water
2 tablespoons vinegar
1 tablespoon Worcestershire/ Pickapeppa sauce
¼ oz. garlic powder
¼ oz. onion powder
½ cup paprika
¼ cup lemon juice

2 tablespoons brown sugar
½ cup chili/tomato sauce
½ teaspoon paprika
1 teaspoon black pepper
1 teaspoon prepared mustard
* hot pepper sauce to taste

Season ribs with mixture of salt, oregano, garlic, onion and paprika. Rub in to meat well. Place ribs in moderate oven with a small amount of water, and cover. Cook for approximately ½ hour until almost tender. Remove from oven and cool. Place ribs on rack over coals, and turn continually until done (approximately 10 minutes). Make sauce by combining all ingredients and simmering for 10 minutes. Just a few minutes before removing from rack, brush ribs with sauce.
Serves 4.

BARBECUED STANDING RIBS (BEEF)

8   10 lbs. ribs
*   salt
*   black pepper
*   garlic powder

SAUCE
14 ozs. ketchup
½ cup white vinegar
1 teaspoon sugar
1/8 teaspoon salt
½ teaspoon cumin
1 teaspoon coriander
1/8 teaspoon paprika
1/8 teaspoon saffron
¼ teaspoon ground ginger
1 red pepper, finely chopped

Season ribs liberally with salt, pepper, garlic powder; let stand overnight. When ready to cook, skewer beef, and cook over coals, turning very slowly, for about 2-3 hours. Meanwhile, combine sauce ingredients, simmer 15 minutes. Baste ribs with sauce only 15 minutes before removing from coals.
Serves 15 people.
To add an extra special touch, orange juice can be added to the basting mixture.

BARBECUED STEAK

2-2½ lbs. sirloin steak
8 ozs. olive oil
¼ cup soy sauce
*   salt to taste
*   black pepper
1 cup tomato sauce
2 tablespoons brown sugar
1 green pepper, cut in chunks
1 onion, sliced

Season steak with salt and pepper. Combine other ingredients, pour over steak. Marinate in refrigerator 4 hours or overnight, turning occasionally. Broil steak.
Serves 4.

BEEF LIVER IN BARBECUE SAUCE

1 lb. beef liver cut in ¼″ slices
2 tablespoons butter or margarine
1 cup sliced onions
½ cup green sweet pepper, cut up
1 tablespoon vinegar
*   salt and black pepper
1 tablespoon Pickapeppa sauce
1 teaspoon sugar
1 teaspoon prepared mustard
¼ cup tomato ketchup
½ teaspoon hot pepper sauce

Start heating oven to 325°F. Cut liver slices in half crosswise. Place half of slices side by side, in covered, shallow baking dish; sprinkle lightly with salt and pepper. Saute onion and sweet pepper in butter or margarine and arrange half on liver. Mix vinegar with next five ingredients with rest of liver then rest of sauce. Bake uncovered for 10 minutes.
Makes 4 servings. The family will need no encouragement to try this dish.

CHRISTMAS HAM WITH BARBECUE SAUCE

1 12-15 lbs. ham
1 cup brown sugar

2 tablespoons mustard
1 cup sherry

Preheat oven to 325°F. Bake ham, allowing 25 minutes per pound. When ham is almost done, remove from oven, score, and add cloves. Make a mixture of brown sugar and mustard, then add sherry. Mixture should be like a thick paste. Coat thickly over ham, then bake for another ½ hour.

SMOKED PORK CHOPS, BAKED WITH JIFFY BARBECUE SAUCE

6 smoked pork chops
1 can whole kernel corn
1 egg, well beaten
1 cup chopped celery

1 onion, chopped
2 tablespoons oil
1 ounce margarine
1 green sweet pepper, chopped

Saute celery, onion and sweet green pepper in margarine, and mix with corn & egg. Brown chops lightly in oil, drain and arrange in a casserole. Cover with the corn mixture and pour sauce (see page 54) all over. Bake covered at 350°F for one hour. Remove cover during last 10 minutes.

ORANGE GRILLED FISH

2 lbs. firm white fish

MARINADE
4 tablespoons soy sauce
2 tablespoons tomato ketchup
2 tablespoons chopped parsley

½ cup orange juice
* grated rind of ½ orange
* salt and blackpepper

Cut the fish into 1" pieces. Mix the ingredients for the marinade together, beating well. Pour over the fish and leave to marinate for 1 hour. Drain the fish and thread on six skewers. Grill over hot coals for about 8 minutes, then turn and grill for a further 7 minutes. Baste with the marinade during cooking.
Serves 6.

SHRIMP WITH COLD BARBECUE SAUCE

2 lbs. fresh shrimp	¼ teaspoon hot pepper sauce
½ cup finely chopped celery	5 tablespoons horseradish
1 stalk skellion	2 tablespoons prepared mustard
6 tablespoons olive oil	¼ teaspoon paprika
3 tablespoons lemon juice	¾ teaspoon salt
¼ cup ketchup	½ teaspoon white pepper
1 clove garlic	

Clean tnen poach shrimp. To prepare sauce: rub bowl with garlic, then combine other ingredients. Marinate shrimp in sauce for an hour. Serve chilled on a bed of lettuce.

SPICY ROAST BEEF BARBECUE

Roasted Irish potatoes, when done liberally drenched with butter or margarine, and maybe roasted ears of sweet corn, would be perfect accompaniments. To cool things off, how about a big cabbage slaw, dressed with Mayonnaise, sprinkled with paprika?

1 (4 - 5) Beef rump roast, rolled and tied	½ teaspoon Pimento
½ cup butter	½ teaspoon coriander
1 cup vinegar	¼ teaspoon chili powder
½ teaspoon dry mustard	1 tablespoon lemon juice
1 tablespoon minced onion	1/3 cup brown sugar
1 tablespoon Pickapeppa Sauce	* salt and pepper to taste

Leave roast at room temperature for at least on hour. Start the fire in the barbecue, and let the charcoal bed burn until charcoal turns ash gray in colour. Tap the gray ash from the coals with fire tongs. After you start the fire, skewer the roast on the spit rod, through the centre of the roast. (If it is not centred properly, the spit will not turn.) Inset holding forks. When the fire is ready, start to brown the roast. While the roast is browning, combine the sauce ingredients in a saucepan, and heat until the butter melts. Makes about 2 cups. When roast is an even brown on all sides start to baste with the sauce, basting every 20 minutes until done.
(See Cooking Chart)

BREAD AND BUTTER PICKLES

- 1 qrt. sliced cucumbers
- 2 sliced onions
- 1 sliced green pepper
- 1 chopped clove garlic
- 1 cup sugar
- ½ teaspoon dry mustard
- * pinch of salt
- * vinegar and spices

Place onions, cucumbers, pepper, garlic and salt in a pan. Cover with ice cubes and let stand for 2 hours. Drain.

Combine other ingredients and pour over onion mixture. Heat to boil for a few minutes only. Seal while still hot in jars. Makes approx. 4 jars.

CORN RELISH

- 12 young corn ears
- 3 peppers (remove seeds)
- 1½ cups sugar
- 2 tablespoons salt
- 2 teaspoons flour
- 4 cups vinegar
- 4 onions
- * mustard to taste

Remove corn from the cob. Put onions and pepper through a mincer and mix with corn. Cover with 3 cups of vinegar.

To remaining cup of vinegar add sugar, salt, flour and mustard to make a paste.

Add this to vegetable mixture and bring to a slow boil for 30 minutes.

Pour into hot jars and seal.

HOT PEPPERS AND SHALLOTS

6 hot peppers
2 cups white vinegar
* shallots to fill 2 jars
1 clove
* salt
* pimento grains

Slice peppers and remove seeds. Peel and wash shallots. Fill jars with shallots and hot pepper slices.
Boil vinegar with spices and salt. Pour over peppers and shallots and seal.

MANGO CHUTNEY

2 ozs. green ginger
2 lbs. brown sugar
1 lb. green mangoes — peel and slice
½ lb. raisins
1 tablespoon soya sauce
1 oz. garlic powder
2 ozs. salt
1 sliced hot pepper
1 sliced onion

Crush the ginger. Mix all ingredients and bring to a boil. Simmer gently until chutney is thick and syrupy. Correct seasoning.

RED DEVIL

6 peppers, seeded and diced
3 diced onions
1 pint vinegar
1 teaspoon nutmeg
* pinch of salt

Put hot peppers and onions through a mincer. Combine with vinegar, nutmeg and salt and bring to a boil.
Bottle when cool.

TO PRESERVE FRESH TOMATOES

Choose firm, ripe, small tomatoes without blemish. Put them into a jar with a large mouth. Fill jar with oil (corn oil preferably) so that tomatoes are covered with a layer of oil 1" deep. On top of oil pour a little brandy or rum and seal.

PICKLED WATERMELON

2 lbs. sugar
2 quarts water
¼ cup salt
1 pint vinegar
* peel of watermelon

4 cloves
1 piece hot pepper
* pieces of cinnamon stick (or grated nutmeg)

Peel off outer green skin of watermelon and chop the white flesh into pieces. Cover with water and salt and simmer until tender.

Bring remaining ingredients to a boil for 10 minutes. Add tender melon to this and continue to simmer until melon is transparent. Pack in jars. Approx. 4 jars.

VEGETABLE RELISH

6 carrots
1 pepper, seeds removed
2 onions
2 chochos

1 cucumber
6 olives
2 cups water

Chop carrots, peppers, onions, chochos, cucumbers and olives, add water to cover. Bring to a boil to tenderize. Drain.

DRESSING
½ cup oil
1 cup vinegar
2 tablespoon ketchup

1 tablespoon hot pepper sauce
* salt to taste

Mix dressing and bring to a boil. Pour dressing over the vegetables, which have been packed in sterilized jars. Makes 4 jars.

GARLIC VINEGAR

Steep garlic cloves, which have been pricked with a pin, in vinegar for 10 days. Use for salad dressings.

HERB VINEGARS

Various herb vinegars can be made by loosely packing a jar with a combination of herbs and filling with vinegar.

Stand jar in a saucepan of water and bring to a boil slowly. Then allow to cool. After 2 weeks vinegar will be ready for use.

PEPPER WINE

Fill ¾ bottle with either cherry or bird peppers. Fill up with sherry or rum. Allow to stand for about one week before using.

Jellies & Jams

PINEAPPLE JAM

- 1 pineapple
- * sugar
- * nutmeg

Peel and grate the pineapple.
To each lb. of pineapple pulp, add ¾ lb. of sugar. Add nutmeg to taste.
Boil and stir until mixture thickens and sugar is melted. Seal in jars whilst hot. Makes approx. 3 jars.

PUMPKIN JAM

- 3 lbs. pumpkin
- 2 lbs. sugar
- 1 lime
- 1 orange
- * salt

Peel and cut pumpkin into slices, then dice and pack in a jar. Add sugar.
Cover and stand for 12 hours. Drain off liquid and boil until syrupy. Add pumpkin, sliced lime and orange. Stir in a pinch of salt. Boil up, and cook until clear.
Seal in jars. Makes approx. 6 jars.

TOMATO JAM

- 8 tomatoes peeled and chopped
- 2 tablespoons lime juice
- 4 cups sugar
- 2 tablespoons chopped raisins
- ½ teaspoon all spice

Simmer tomatoes for 10 minutes. Add all ingredients except sugar and bring to a boil. Add sugar and continue to boil until sugar melts and mixture thickens. Skim and cool.

CALF'S FOOT JELLY

calves feet
qrts. cold water
whites and crushed shells of eggs
juice of 3 limes
juice of 1 orange

2 cups sugar
1 pint sherry
½ teaspoon nutmeg
½ cup water

Clean feet well and put into a pan of cold water. Bring slowly to a boil and simmer for hours. Set aside to cool overnight. In the morning skim jelly from the top and discard diment on bottom.

Put on heat and melt slowly. Add egg whites beaten to a froth, the crushed shells, nut- eg, sugar and fruit juices. Boil hard for 20 minutes without stirring.

Add 1 cup of water and let come to a boil again. Reduce heat and let simmer. covered or about 30 minutes.

Dip a flannel jelly bag into boiling water. Hang it up with a bowl underneath. Pour ly into bag and let it drip. The bag must not be touched or jelly will cloud.

Turn jelly into a mould. Stir in wine and put in a cool place.

SEA GRAPE JELLY

lbs. sea grapes
pints water

* sugar

Add grapes to water and bring to a boil. Stir with a wooden spoon and crush fruit hilst stirring. Boil about 20 minutes.

Drip through a sieve without stirring. Measure this juice and for every cup of liquid d an equal amount of sugar. Return sugar and liquid to heat and boil rapidly. Skim. oil until a little tested on a plate will jell.

Pour into jars, and cool before sealing. Makes approx. 4-5 jars.

ORANGE JELLY AND GUAVA JELLY

lbs. sliced guavas or 7 cups diced oranges

7 pints water (boil 30 minutes)
* sugar

These are made to the same formula as seagrape jelly (see above).

Strain and measure juice in each instance, and add an equal amount of sugar. Boil until quid jells — Pour into jars. Makes approx. 4-5 jars.

BLENDER GRAPEFRUIT MARMALADE

4 grapefruits
2 limes
1½ cups water

5 cups sugar
1/8 teaspoon soda
1 oz. gelatin powder

Lightly peel and seed grapefruit. Chop two and put into a blender with ½ cup water Mince. Add soda to this and boil for 30 minutes.

Cut up remaining 2 grapefruits and limes discarding seeds. Add to ½ cup water and mince in blender. Add this to cooked mixture with rest of water and boil for 30 minutes

Add sugar and stir and boil for 10-15 minutes, being careful to stir frequently to avoid burning and to melt sugar.

Add dissolved gelatin to marmalade when it has cooled slightly. Should make 4 jars

---

ORANGE MARMALADE

4 large seville oranges
2 teaspoons salt

* sugar

Wash oranges and peel lightly. Cut into quarters, removing pips and pulp. Cover pips and pulp with water and let stand overnight. Slice (or cut with scissors) the peel very thinly and add a little salt. Cover with water and soak overnight.

The next morning bring peel to a boil and boil until tender. Strain liquid from pips and pulp and add to the fruit mixture. Measure this and add sugar equal to this quantity

Boil up again, simmer and stir until sugar melts and liquid thickens. Be careful not to burn, so at this point cook on a low flame.

When mixture jells, skim and remove and pour into jars.

GUAVA CHEESE

* ripe guavas (whatever number desired)

* sugar

Wash guavas, cut in half, cover with water and boil until tender. Rub through a sieve, weigh the pulp, and add an equal quantity of sugar.

Boil until mixture shrinks from sides of pot. Stir all the time to prevent burning.

When a little dropped into water forms a ball, pour into a shallow dish. Cool and cut into squares when firm.

GUAVA BUTTER

Wash and cut guavas in half; using a pointed teaspoon remove seeds. Cut into pieces and place in a pot. Add water until you can see it between the guava pieces. Cook over moderate heat until tender. Strain and sieve. Measure pulp and add equal measurement of sugar. Add lime juice to taste, if desired. Cook until mixture is thick, stirring frequently to prevent scorching.

Desserts

AMBROSIA

4 oranges peeled and sliced
1 small shredded coconut
4 tablespoons wine
½ cup pomegranate seeds
* sugar

Pile fruit in alternate layers into a bowl, sprinkle with sugar, coconut and wine. End with a layer of pomegranate seeds.

BANANAS IN BATTER

3 ripe bananas
½ cup rum
1 tablespoon sugar
1 teaspoon lime juice
3 ozs. flour
* oil
1 oz. sugar
½ oz. butter
9 tablespoon milk
1 teaspoon baking powder
1 egg

Peel bananas and cut into thick chunks. Soak in rum, sugar and lime juice.
Mix remaining ingredients except the oil. Dip banana chunks into the batter using a perforated spoon. Fry lightly in hot oil.

RIPE BANANA PIE

2 sliced bananas
1 package lime jello — prepared as instructions
* cherries
* shredded coconut (optional)

Place sliced bananas in a prebaked pie shell. Cover with cooked lime jello mixture. Chill.

COCONUT TRIFLE

1 lb. flour
½ lb. butter
1 teaspoon baking powder
¾ cup milk

2 eggs
1½ cups sugar
1 coconut, grated

Cream butter and sugar until fluffy. Add eggs and continue beating. Add coconut, then flour and milk alternately and lastly baking powder and blend well. Pour into greased pan and bake in 350 degrees oven for about 40 minutes.

COCONUT CREAM PIE

Pastry

2¼ cups sifted flour
1 cup shortening
water

1 teaspoon salt
2 tablespoons butter

In a bowl, mix flour and salt. With pastry blender or 2 knives cut 2/3 of shortening int flour until it appears like corn meal. Cut in the remainder of shortening and the butter unt it appears more grainy. Sprinkle cold water until dough comes together. lightly form th dough into a smooth ball. Roll out and line an 8 inch pan.

Filling

1 medium size coconut, peeled and grated
¾ lb. butter
2 eggs

1 teaspoon vanilla, rum or almond extract
1 cup sugar
2 cups milk

Cream butter and sugar. Add eggs, one at a time, beating after each addition. Add mil and coconut and mix well. Pour into unbaked pie shell. Bake at 350 degrees for 40 to 5 minutes.

COCONUT GIZZADAS

1 lb. brown sugar
¼ pt. water
1 grated coconut
½ teaspoon nutmeg

2 cups flour
¼ teaspoon salt
¼ cup margarine
* iced water to blend

Make a syrup of sugar and water. Add coconut and nutmeg. Mix well. Cool and fill pastry shells made as follows.
Mix flour and salt, cut in margarine and water. Roll out and cut into circles. Mould into cases and pinch up edges. Fill with mixture and bake in a 400°F oven until pastry shells are golden brown.

COCONUT MOULD

1 tablespoon gelatin powder
¼ cup warm water
3 cups coconut cream
1 tin condensed milk

Dissolve gelatin in warm water. Mix with coconut cream and condensed milk. Heat through to melt gelatin, but do not boil or mixture will curdle. Cool and chill.

CHOCOLATE MOUSSE

Per person
1 egg
1 oz. plain chocolate
1 tablespoon black coffee
1 tablespoon rum

Melt chocolate over low heat.
Separate eggs, reserving whites, beat yolks and stir into melted chocolate mixed with coffee and rum. Whip egg whites and fold into mixture.
Put into individual glasses and chill.

BRANDIED PUMPKIN PIE

1 unbaked 9 inch pastry shell
2 cups cooked pumpkin
2/3 cup brown sugar, packed
½ teaspoon cinnamon
½ teaspoon ginger
¼ teaspoon freshly grated nutmeg
¼ teaspoon ground cloves
2 eggs, slightly beaten
1 can evaporated milk
¼ cup brandy

In large mixing bowl combine pumpkin, brown sugar, salt and spices. Blend in eggs, evaporated milk, and the brandy. Pour into pastry shell. Bake at 400 degrees F. for 45 minutes or until knife inserted half way between the centre and outside edge comes out clean. Cool. Just before serving, prepare sweetened whipped cream topping flavoured with brandy or substitute a topping mix prepared according to package directions, substituting 2 tablespoons brandy for 2 tablespoons of the liquid called for on the package. Garnish generously with topping. Sprinkle lightly with freshly grated nutmeg.

TROPICAL FRUIT SALAD

1 ripe pineapple or melon
* variety of diced fruits, as desired
* brandy, optional

Cut off the top of a ripe pineapple or use a melon cut into 2 parts. Scoop out flesh and mix with diced fruits — as many varieties as desired. Toss with 2 tablespoons brandy if desired.
Return to shell and chill. Fresh lychee and mangos can be added.

GUAVA MOUSSE

1 cup tinned guava nectar
1 tablespoon gelatin powder
2 tablespoons water
1 cup whipped cream

Dissolve gelatin in water and add to guava nectar. Heat slowly to melt gelatin. Cool slightly before adding the whipped cream. Set in individual glasses. Chill to serve.

GUAVA PIE

CRUST
1½ cups flour
2 tablespoons sugar
1¼ teaspoons baking powder
3 tablespoons butter
¾ cup milk
* a pinch of salt

Mix flour, sugar, baking powder and salt. Cut butter into this and blend until mixutre looks like cornmeal. Stir in milk.

Knead on a floured board for 1 minute. Divide dough into 2 balls. Roll out bottom crust, cut and fit into a greased pie dish. Put in filling of guava slices with some syrup.

Cover with remaining dough. Brush over with milk and make one or two slits in the pastry. Bake in a 350° oven for about 30 minutes.

FILLING

6 ripe guavas (when in season)
  or use tinned guavas
* water
* sugar

Peel fresh guavas, cut in half and scoop out seeds. Cover with water, add sugar and boil slowly until fruit is tender and a syrup has formed. Fill crust.

LIME PIE

2 egg yolks
4 ozs. condensed milk
¾ cup lime juice
* salt
6 tablespoons sugar
3 egg whites
1 baked pie shell

Beat yolks, stir in milk and add lime juice gradually. Beat well.

Whip egg whites with a pinch of salt and fold into mixture.

Pour into a baked pie shell and cover with meringue made with 3 stiffly beaten egg whites and 6 tablespoons sugar.

Bake in a preheated oven for 10 minutes — or until meringue is a golden colour.

GUAVA DUFF

3 cups flour	3 teaspoons baking powder
¾ cup butter-flavoured crisco	¾ cup milk
1 teaspoon salt	8 large guavas
1 egg beaten	1 tablespoon cinnamon
2 tablespoons sugar	1 tablespoon ground spice

Wash and peel guavas, cut in half and remove seeds. Dice the fruit and strain seeds through the sieve to remove juice and set aside. Place the diced guava, sugar, cinnamon and allspice in a pot on low flame. Cook stirring gravy until tender; allow to cool. Sift together the flour, salt and baking powder. Cut in the shortening with pastry blender or knife until the mixture resembles crumbs. Pour in the milk; cooked guava; add the egg and mix to a soft dough. Knead until smooth. Wrap dough easily in greased foil paper. Wrap in additional foil to prevent water from entering it. Boil dough for ½ hour in a large pot half full of boiling water. Serve sliced duff with sauce.

Sauce

Reserve guava juice from seeds. Cream butter and sugar together. Add egg and juice from guava seeds. Beat well; serve over sliced duff.

MANGO PIE

3 cups peeled and very thinly sliced mango	1–2 tablespoons lime juice
1 teaspoon cinnamon	1 teaspoon freshly grated nutmeg
1 cup sugar	2 tablespoons butter or margarine

Place 1 layer of mangoes in a pie shell and sprinkle with half the sugar, or lime juice and spices. Add remaining slices of mango, sugar, spices, lime juice and dot with bits of butter or margarine. Cover or criss cross with pie crust. Bake about 45 minutes at 350°F.

BAHAMIAN MINCE PIE

1 unbaked 9-inch pie shell	1 cup apples, cut fine
½ cup raisins	juice and rind of 1 lemon
½ cup dried prunes	juice of 1 orange
1 cup honey	½ cup dates, chopped
3 tablespoons flour	

Combine ingredients and mix well; place into unbaked 9-inch pie shell. Cover with top crust and stick holes in top to let steam escape. Bake in moderate oven (350 degrees F.) for 55 minutes.

ORANGE SORBET

1½ pts. water
5 ozs. sugar
4 oranges

1 lime
1 glass white wine
1 egg white

Bring the sugar and water to a boil, dissolve and reduce.
Add the grated rind of 1 orange, and the juice of 4 oranges and 1 lime. Bring to a boil strain and cool
Semi-freeze. Whisk egg white briskly and add along with wine to mixture. Freeze until mushy and serve in parfait glasses.

BAKED BANANA

4 bananas
2 tablespoons brown sugar
¼ cup coconut (thickly shredded)
1 ounce banana liqueur

4 tablespoons guava jelly
2 tablespoons butter
4 tablespoons whip topping

Peel bananas and cut in half lengthwise then arrange lengthwise in a buttered pyrex dish. Place guava jelly on top. Sprinkle with sugar. Dot with butter. Cover with foil. Bake at 350 degrees for 10 minutes. Mix coconut and topping together. Remove banana from oven and place in a hot dish, pour liqueur lightly over. Add coconut milk and serve.

RUM COFFEE JELLY

2 tablespoons gelatin
2 cups of hot strong coffee
½ cup sugar
2 tablespoons lime juice

3 tablespoons rum
2 cups sour cream
1 cup brown sugar
½ teaspoon cinnamon

Soften gelatin in ½ cup of cold water. Add hot coffee and sugar and stir until gelatin is dissolved. Add lime juice and rum.
Pour into an 8" dish and chill until firm. Cut into cubes and serve a sauce made by beating together sour cream, sugar and cinnamon until sugar dissolves.

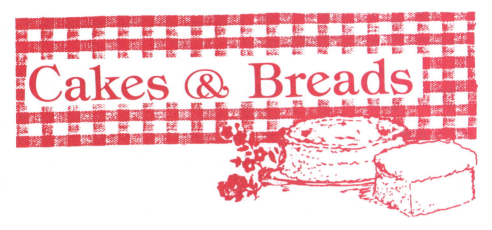

Cakes & Breads

BASIC BREAD DOUGH

2½ cups flour
1 teaspoon dry yeast
½ cup warm water
* pinch of salt

2 tablespoons melted butter
5 tablespoons cold milk
1 egg beaten into 1 tablespoon milk
2 tablespoons flour

Sift flour and salt. Dissolve yeast in ½ cup of warm water. Combine with butter and milk. Cover bowl and set aside to rise for 2 hours.
Put 2 tablespoons flour on table and pat dough to ½" thickness. Cut dough into 2 pieces and roll from corner to corner like a jelly roll.
Brush with egg and milk and slash surface at intervals. Place in bread loaf pans and bake 15 minutes in a fast oven, then lower to 350° and bake 15 minutes more.

BANANA BREAD

1 cup sugar
¼ cup margarine or butter
3 crushed, ripe bananas
2 cups flour

1 unbeaten egg
1 teaspoon baking powder
½ teaspoon soda
* vanilla flavouring

Cream sugar and butter. Add bananas and mix well. Add egg and dry ingredients and vanilla. Beat well.
Bake in a greased, paper lined loaf tin at 350° for 50 minutes. This freezes well.

EGG BREAD

1 pk. yeast
4 cups flour
1 cup warm water
1 tablespoon oil

2 teaspoons sugar
2 eggs (beaten)
1 egg yolk

Soak yeast in warm water for 5 minutes. Sift flour, salt and sugar together. Add 1½ cups flour to the yeast and beat. Cover and allow to rise about 30 minutes.
Add the 2 eggs and remaining flour and oil to dough. Knead. Place in a bowl to rise for 2 hours.
Knead dough again. Divide into 3 strands and braid, turning ends under. Place on a greased sheet and let rise for 1 hour.
Preheat 400°. Brush the top with egg yolk. Bake for 10-15 minutes. Reduce oven to 350° and bake 30 minutes. Bread should be golden brown on top.

ORANGE BREAD

1 cup minced orange peel
1 cup orange juice
2½ cups of sugar
1 beaten egg
3½ cups flour

1 cup milk
½ teaspoon melted butter
2 teaspoons baking powder
* pinch of salt

Combine orange peel and juice and boil until peel is tender. Add 1½ cups sugar, and boil slowly until thick and syrupy. Cool.
Mix egg, 1 cup sugar, butter and milk. Sift flour with baking powder and salt. Add mixture and stir. Add orange mixture to dough and blend well.
Pour into 2 loaf tins which have been greased and floured. Bake at 350° for 40 minutes. This is good toasted with cheese spread.

PUMPKIN BREAD

3 cups sugar
1 cup oil
4 eggs

1 cup boiled, crushed pumpkin
3 cups flour

Grease and flour 2 loaf pans. Mix all ingredients together in a large bowl. Pour into pans.
Bake 1 hour at 350°. Cool for 10 minutes in the pan. Wrap in foil and store in the refrigerator.

SODA BREAD

1 lb. flour
1 cup warm milk

2 tablespoons soda
1 tablespoon salt

Mix all ingredients and knead to a soft dough. Divide into 2 loaves.
Brush with milk and dredge lightly with flour. Bake for 30-40 minutes or until lightly brown on top in a 425° oven.

BAKING POWDER BISCUITS

2 cups flour
2½ teaspoons baking powder
1/3 cup margarine

¾ cup milk
* salt

Sift together flour and baking powder. Cut margarine into the flour mixture with a fork. Add milk and salt. Knead and roll out to ½" thickness.
Cut into circles and bake on an ungreased sheet for 15 minutes in a hot oven, 400° - 450°.

BANANA MUFFINS

6½ ozs. flour
1 tablespoon corn flour
2 ozs. butter
3 ozs. sugar

1 egg
3 crushed bananas
1 teaspoon baking powder
½ teaspoon soda and a pinch of salt

Sift together, flour, cornflour, baking powder, soda and salt. Cream butter and sugar. Beat egg and mix into creamed mixture.
Add dry ingredients and crushed bananas alternately. Do not beat, but mix in well. Bake in greased muffin containers in 400° oven for 20 minutes.

JOHNNY CAKE – CORN BREAD

7/8 cup flour
¼ cup sugar
4 teaspoon baking powder
½ teaspoon salt

1 cup corn meal
1 egg beaten
1 cup milk
¼ cup butter/margarine

Sift together flour, sugar, baking powder and salt. Blend in corn meal. Combine egg, milk and butter or margarine. Make a well in centre of dry ingredients and add the egg mixture. Stir until blended. Pour into greased 8" square cake pan. Bake in preheated 375 degree F. oven for 23 – 30 minutes. Serve hot with butter, jelly, honey or preserves.

JOURNEY CAKE

2 cups flour
2 teaspoon baking powder
1 teaspoon salt

1 tablespoon sugar
1 tablespoon shortening
water to make a firm dough

Place all ingredients except water in mixing bowl and using spoon or hands, mix thoroughly. Add just enough water to make a firm dough. Turn out board and knead until smooth. Let stand 10 minutes. Place in a hot frying pan which has been well greased and flatten to fit the frypan. Fry at medium heat until brown and crusty, turning several times. Then lower flame and finish cooking about 15 minutes.

HOT COCONUT BREAD

1 dry coconut, grated
2 eggs
½ cup vegetable shortening
2 cups evaporated milk

1 cup sugar
1 teaspoon salt
4 cups flour
1 tablespoon baking powder

Place coconut in mixing bowl and add eggs, shortening, evaporated milk, sugar and salt. Mix together and slowly add flour, and baking powder. Beat well. Pour into greased pan — preferably iron. Bake slowly at 325–350°F. for 20 minutes to ½ hour or until brown and toothpick inserted in centre comes out clean.

A JAMAICAN BUN

1 lb. flour
2 ozs. butter
2 ozs. margarine
2 ozs. raisins
2 ozs. mixed peel
2 eggs

6 ozs. currants
½ lb. brown sugar
½ teaspoon nutmeg
½ teaspoon baking powder
* enough milk to make a batter

Blend butter and margarine into flour. Add baking powder, sugar and nutmeg. Add fruit to flour.
Beat the eggs and pour into the dry mixture adding enough milk to make a batter. Pour into a greased loaf tin and bake 1½ hours in a slow oven, about 300°.
Chopped cherries and some lime rind may be added to the mixture if desired.

COCONUT LOAF CAKE

½ cup butter
1½ cups sugar
2 + 2/3 cups flour
¾ cup milk

2 eggs
4 teaspoons baking powder
1 cup grated coconut
1 teaspoon vanilla

Cream butter and ½ of the sugar. Beat eggs with rest of sugar and combine the mixture.
Mix in flour and baking powder adding milk alternately with the dry ingredients. Add coconut and vanilla. Bake 1 hour in a 350° oven.

GUAVA LAYER CAKE

½ lb. margarine
1 cup sugar
2 eggs
2 cups flour
1 cup milk

2 teaspoons baking powder
¼ teaspoon nutmeg
½ teaspoon vanilla
* stewed guava slices, or use tinned

Cream margarine, sugar and eggs. Beat well. Add flour, baking powder and nutmeg. Pour in milk to which vanilla has been added.

Bake in two 9" layer tins for 30 minutes in a 350° oven. Cool and remove from pans. Spread guava slices between the layers. Sprinkle sugar lightly on top.

Stewed mangoes may be used in the same manner.

ORANGE CAKE

3 oranges
2 eggs
¾ cup sugar
2 cups flour

½ teaspoon soda and a tip of salt
1 cup butter
¼ cup grated orange rind

Squeeze juice from oranges to make 1 cup and reserve. Cream butter and sugar and add eggs one at a time, beating continuously.

Add flour, salt and soda, which have been sifted together. Continue to beat the mixture. Add ¼ cup of orange rind and the juice.

Pour into a greased 13" x 9" pan and bake in a moderate oven until firm.

RUM CAKE

½ cup butter
1 cup sugar
3 beaten eggs
¼ teaspoon salt
½ teaspoon baking powder
3 cups flour
* mixed spices

¼ cup milk
¼ cup molasses
2 cups peanuts (crushed)
1 lb. raisins
½ cup rum
* pinch of soda

Cream butter, sugar and eggs. Mix flour, baking powder, salt and spices. Add this to butter mixture and blend.

Add milk, soda and molasses, and add lastly crushed nuts, raisins and rum.

Bake in a loaf tin 300° for 2 hours.

COCONUT COOKIES

¾ cup sugar
¼ lb. butter
1½ cups flour

1 tsp. baking powder
1½ cups grated coconut
1 beaten egg

    Cream butter and sugar. Add flour and baking powder. Mix well then add grated coconut and egg.
    Mix to a paste. Drop onto a greased cookie sheet by teaspoonfuls. Bake at 350° for 15 minutes. Makes approx. 2 doz.

GUAVA JELLY COOKIES

4 ozs. butter
2 ozs. sugar
1 egg yolk
½ teaspoon vanilla
4 ozs. flour

1 egg white
3 tablespoons chopped nuts
3 tablespoons guava jelly
* pinch of salt

    Cream butter and sugar and beat in yolk and vanilla. Combine flour and salt and add to mixture.
    Divide and shape into balls. Roll in egg white and then in nuts. Press a hole into each cookie and insert guava jelly.
    Bake with jelly uppermost, on a sheet for 20 minutes in a moderate oven. Makes approx. 1 doz.

SWEET POTATO COOKIES

1½ cups flour
2 tablespoons brown sugar
4 teaspoons baking powder
5 tablespoons butter

1 cup crushed, boiled, sweet potato
½ cup of milk
* cinnamon

    Combine all but milk and potatoes and mix until crumbly. Stir in crushed potatoes and milk.
    Spoon batter on to a sheet.
    Bake in a quick oven.
    Split and serve with honey and butter. Makes approx. 1 doz.

Beverages

MATRIMONY

3 star apples
2 oranges

4 tablespoons condensed milk
* nutmeg

Remove starapple pulp. Peel orange and remove sections, discarding seeds.
Mix together, sweeten with condensed milk, and flavour with grated nutmeg. Chill.

NASEBERRY NECTAR

6 naseberries peeled and seeded
1 cup sugar

1 cup water
* juice of 1 orange

Put all ingredients through a blender, strain and serve chilled.

PLANTATION RUM PUNCH

3 ozs. any rum
1 oz. lime juice

1 teaspoon honey
* nutmeg

Mix together and pour over cracked ice. Add a sprinkle of nutmeg.

SORREL APPETIZER

Preparation of Sorrel:

Strip sorrel leaves from bud and wash. Put water to boil. Place sorrel leaves and crushed fresh ginger into bowl and cover with boiling water.

Leave overnight to soak. Strain and add rum and sugar to taste. Serve over crushed ice.

1 lb. prepared sorrel	6 pints boiling water
2 ozs. grated green ginger	2 cloves

Mix ingredients together, cover and leave overnight. Strain and add rum and sugar to taste. Serve over crushed ice.

SOURSOP PUNCH

1 ripe soursop	* condensed milk to taste
4 glasses water	* vanilla or rum to flavour

Peel and crush soursop, removing seeds. Stir in water and strain. Add milk and flavouring. Serve ice cold.

STARAPPLE APPETIZER

6 star apples (use pulp only)	2 teaspoons lime juice
2 tablespoons rum	* angostura bitters
2 tablespoons sugar	

Cut star apples in half, remove pulp and mix with rum, sugar and lime juice. Add a few drops of angostura bitters. Serve chilled in fruit glasses.

For a full range of Tropical Beverages see
"Caribbean Cocktails & Mixed Drinks" by Mike Henry

CHRISTMAS CITRUS PUNCH

cups grapefruit juice
cups ortanique juice
cups orange juice
bottles soda water

¾ cup honey (or to taste)
1 whole orange, unpeeled
12 cloves

Stick the cloves into the orange and bake in a warm oven until hard.

Put the honey into a large bowl and add the fruit juices gradually, stirring so that the honey is completely dissolved. Add the baked orange. Allow the mixture to stand for two hours at least.

When ready to serve, place a block of ice in a large bowl and pour the punch over it. Use a ladle to pour the punch over the ice repeatedly until it is completely chilled. Add the soda water and serve.

Rum can be added to this punch while it is standing. It can also be garnished with sprigs of mint.

Brunch

1. Hot Buttered Rum or Carrot Punch*
   Banana King Fish
   Baked Black Crabs
   Coconut Gizzadas
   Mango Fool

2. Boo Boo's Special*
   Curried Crawfish
   Sweet Pepper Salad
   Guava Cheese
   Guava Jelly Cookies
   Coffee a la Mike

3. Policeman Glow*
   Crab Fitters
   Avocado and Grapefruit
   Callaloo Salad
   Matrimony

4. Bloody Mary*
   Escoveitch of Grouper
   Johnny Cake
   Banana Muffin served with butter and orange marmalade
   Jamaican Coffee

5. Coffee Coconut*
   Crab Fritters
   Cucumber and Sour Cream Salad garnished with sweet peppers
   Pumpkin Bread served with tomato jam
   Tropical Fruit Salad

6. Sour-Sop Punch*
   Liver with sweet pepper
   Egg Bread served with pineapple jam
   Ambrosia
   Coffee a la Blue Mountain

7. Naked Lady or Hot Barbados Rum Egg Nog*
   Fresh Fruit Plate
   Chicken Souse
   Boiled Fish
   Okra with Tomatoes
   Guava Pie

Lunch

1. Hot Flashes*
   Crawfish Soup
   Bahamian Conch Salad
   Lime Pie

2. Pineapple Cocktails*
   Fish Tea
   Broad Bean Salad
   Beef & Mango in Beer
   Yam Casserole
   Sliced Tomatoes
   Orange Sorbet

3. Air Conditioner*
   Pepper Pot Soup
   Chicken Salad
   Sweet Pepper Salad
   Pumpkin Bread
   Coconut Mould

4. Banana Punch*
   Oysters
   Nassau Chicken with Peas & Rice
   String Bean Salad
   Rum Coffee Jelly

5. Woodpecker*
   Coconut Chips
   Okra Soup
   Crawfish Newburg with mint glazed carrots
   Okra and Rice
   Coconut Cream Pie

6. Special Rum Punch (hot)*
   Crawfish Soup
   Barbecued Steak
   Peas & Rice
   Conch Salad
   Guava Mousse

7. Spanish Town*
   Pumpkin Soup
   Marinated Pork Chops
   Shrimp Salad with Coconut Cream
   Breadfruit Salad
   Coconut Cream Pie

Dinner

1. Desperate Virgin*
   Grapefruit with shrimp & sour cream
   Jamaican Salad
   Conch Soup
   Salmi of Duck
   Pumpkin Puff
   Cho Chos baked with Cheese
   Guava Layer Cake

2. Suffering Bastard*
   Avocado & Grapefruit Salad
   Gungo Pea Soup
   Pork Chops with Pineapple
   Baked Sweet Potatoes
   Coffee Mousse

3. Clarendon Cocktail*
   Crawfish Fritters
   Bahamian Conch Soup
   Curried Lobster
   Okra with rice
   Onion Salad
   Guava Pie

4. Frozen Daiquiri (Stella's Joy)*
   Lobster Salad
   Barbecued Lamb Chops
   Callaloo Bake
   Mint Glazed Carrots
   Orange Ice Box Dessert

5. Pineapple Caribbean*
   Conch Salad
   Barbecued Chicken
   Corn Fritters
   Cauliflower Custard
   Banana Pudding

6. Dry Martini*
   Shrimp Salad with coconut cream
   Cold Thick Cucumber Soup
   Steamed Abaco
   Wild Hog
   Peas & Rice
   Egg Plant with Cheese & Tomatoes
   Carrot Ambrosia
   Ripe Banana Pie

7. West Indian Punch*
   Tropical Salad
   Cho Cho Puree
   King Fish Fillets
   Yam Casserole
   Beans in sour cream sauce
   Lime Pie

---

* See Caribbean Cocktails by Mike Henry

GLOSSARY OF COOKING TERMS

BAIN MARIE	A French cooking utensil similar to a double boiler used to cook over boiling water	Coat	To cover entire surface of food with flour, breadcrumbs, or batter
Bake	To cook by dry heat, usually in an oven	Cream	To combine butter or other shortening with sugar using a wooden spoon or mixer until light and fluffy
Barbecue	Generally refers to food cooked outdoors over an open fire with a spicy sauce	Croutons	Small cubes of fried bread
Baste	To brush or spoon liquid over food while cooking, to keep it moist	Cut in	To mix batter or margarine with dry ingredients, with pastry blender, knives or fork
Batter	Any combination which includes flour, milk, butter, eggs or the like for pancakes, coating, dipping etc.	DEEP FRY	To cook in deep hot fat or oil which covers the food until crisp and golden
		Dice	To cut into small cubes
Beat	To mix with a whisk beater or spoon so as to make the mixture smooth	Disjoint	To separate the joints — of poultry etc.
Blanch	To heat in boiling water or steam for a short period only to loosen skin, remove colour or set colour	Dot	To scatter small bits of butter or margarine over surface of food
		FLAME	To spoon alcoholic fluid over and ignite, to warm the alcohol, and pour flaming over food
Blend	To mix two or more ingredients thoroughly		
Boil	To cook in any liquid at boiling point	Fold in	To use a spoon in a gentle rolling circular action as a means of combining ingredients
Bone	To remove bones from meat, poultry, game and fish		
CHILL	To place in refrigerator until cold	Fry	To cook in hot fat using moderate to high heat

GHEE	Clarified butter, used in curries
Glaze	A thin coating of beaten egg-milk, syrup or aspic which is brushed over pastry, fruits, ham chicken etc.
Grate	To rub food against a grater to form small particles
Grill	To cook by direct heat either over a charcoal fire or under a gas or electric grill unit
JULIENNE	A term for foods cut into thin strips like matches
KNEAD	To work dough with hands until it is of the desired elasticity or consistency
MARINADE	Liquid used for seasoning by soaking usually a mixture of oil, wine and seasonings
Marinate	To soak in a marinade to soften or add flavour
PARBOIL	To boil until partly cooked
Pate	A highly seasoned meat paste
Pit	To remove pit—stone or seed—from fruit
Poach	To cook gently in simmering liquid
Pound	To reduce to small particles or a paste, using a pestle and mortar
Preheat	To turn over to a selected temperature 10 minutes before it is needed
Puree	To press through a fine sieve or put through a food blender to produce a smooth mixture
Reduce	To cook over a high heat, uncovered until it is reduced to desired consistency
ROAST	To cook meat by dry heat in the oven or on a spit
Roux	A mixture of fat and flour cooked slowly, stirring frequently — used to thicken sauces soups etc.
SALMI	A hash — usually of duck
Saute	To fry lightly in a small amount of fat turning and stirring frequently
Scald	To pour boiling water over foods, or bring to boiling.
Score	To cut narrow gashes on the surface of foods
Shred	To cut into fine strips
Simmer	To cook in liquid just below boiling point
Skim	To remove foam, fat or solid substances from the surface of a cooking mixture.
Sliver	To cut into long thin strips
Steam	To cook in vapour rising from boiling water
Stew	A long slow method of cooking in liquid in a covered pan, to tenderize tough meats.
Stir	To blend ingredients with a circular motion

Stock	A liquid containing the flavours, extracts, and nutrients of bones — meat — fish or vegetables, in which they are cooked	Toss	To mix lightly, using a fork and a spoon — i.e. salad chiefly
TOAST	To brown in a toaster, or oven	WHIP	To beat rapidly with hand or electric beater or wire whisk

35 USEFUL COOKING & HOUSEHOLD HINTS

1/3 to 1/2 teaspoon of dried herbs = 1 tablespoon fresh herbs.

Rub ½ lime on your hands or cutting board to remove onion, garlic or fish odours.

To avoid trouble with weevils, keep flour or cornmeal in a glass jar or plastic container the refrigerator.

1 tablespoon oil in water for boiling pastas (macaroni etc.) prevents it from sticking together.

1 lb. coffee brews 40 cups.

For a tender pie crust use less water than is called for.

Dip knife in hot water to slice hard boiled eggs.

1 cup macaroni makes 2 cups of cooked macaroni.

Freeze left over coffee in an icecube tray. When used to chill iced coffee, the cubes will not dilute the coffee.

Parsley rinsed in hot water instead of cold retains more flavour.

Brown sugar will not become lumpy if stored in a jar with a piece of blotting paper fitted to the inside of the jar lid.

If food boils over in the oven, cover with salt to prevent smoking and excessive odour.

Add diced crisp bacon and a dash of nutmeg to cauliflower or cabbage for a gourmet touch.

To keep kettles clean, fill with cold water, add some ammonia and bring to a boil. Rinse well.

Gas ovens must be wiped clean before oven is cold. Racks and shelves must be washed with hot water and washing soda.

Wash pewter with hot water and soap, polish will scratch the surface.

Mildew stains can be removed by soaking overnight in sour milk. Dry in the sun without rinsing. Repeat process if necessary.

To remove a scorch, spread a paste of starch and cold water over the mark. Dry in sun and brush off.

Wash glass windows with crumpled newspaper dipped in cold water, to which has been added a few drops of ammonia.

For wood worms − apply kerosene oil with a brush to the infected area daily for 10 days.

To stop doors creaking rub hinges with soap.

Rust marks can be removed from steel by rubbing with a cut onion.

When washing thermos flasks, add a little vinegar to the water. It removes the musty smell. Do not cork flasks when storing.

To remove stains from china use a rag dipped in cold water and salt.

Before baking have ingredients at room temperature.

To chop sticky dried fruits, heat knife before using.

To prepare nuts, first blanch. Cover with cold water and bring to the boil. Let soak until skin wrinkles then slip the skin off between the fingers.

Parsley freezes well. Cut stems and place bunch in a plastic bag. Thaws easily.

Tear lettuce into pieces instead of cutting to prevent browning.

It is a good idea to make stock from left over bones and keep in the freezer to enhance soups and sauces.

Soak tarnished silver in hot water and ammonia − 1 tablespoon ammonia to 1 quart water.

Sour milk can be made by adding two teaspoons of lime juice to a cup of warm milk, which will curdle.

Moulds should be oiled before they are filled. Custards baked in hot water should be removed and left to stand for 5 minutes to settle before unmoulding. Run knife around the edge. Place a plate over the mould, invert the plate and mould and lift off.

As soon as vegetables are tender drain and plunge into cold water. This sets the colour. Vegetables may be stored and reheated when needed.

Whip cream in a large bowl set in ice. If no cream is available, place a tin of evaporated milk in the freezer for about one hour and then proceed to whip as for cream.
To sweeten, use icing sugar, which is preferable to granulated sugar.

TABLE OF MEASUREMENTS AND MISCELLANEOUS EQUIVALENTS

Dash	=	Less than 1/8 teaspoon
3 teaspoon	=	Tablespoon
4 tablespoons	=	¼ cup
8 tablespoons	=	½ cup
16 tablespoons	=	1 cup
1 cup	=	½ pint
2 cups	=	1 pint
4 cups	=	1 qrt.
2 liquid cups	=	1 lb.
2 pints	=	1 quart
4 quarts	=	1 gallon
1 fluid ounce	=	2 tablespoons
8 fluid ounces	=	1 cup
16 ounces	=	1 pound
1 lb. butter	=	2 cups
1 carrot	=	½ cup chopped
¼ lb. cheese	=	1 cup grated
1 envelope gelatin	=	1 tablespoon
1 teaspoon dried herbs	=	1 tablespoon fresh
juice of 1 lime	=	1 tablespoon
1 medium onion	=	¾ cup chopped
1 medium potato	=	½ cup chopped
1 pk. dry yeast	=	¼ oz.

SOME SUBSTITUTIONS

When you do not have exactly what the recipe calls for, here are some suggestions which are acceptable substitutes.

1 square cooking chocolate	3 tablespoons cocoa + 1 oz. butter
1 cup self raising flour	1 cup plain flour + 2 teaspoons of baking powder
1 cup sour milk	1 tablespoon lime juice or white vinegar + 1 cup milk
1 cup fresh milk	½ cup evaporated milk + ½ cup water
1 cup sour cream	1 cup warm milk + 1 tablespoon lime juice or white vinegar. Stirred to a thick consistency
Yeast compressed (1 oz.)	2 Teaspoons active dry yeast
1 fresh garlic clove	¼ teaspoon garlic powder
fresh green root ginger, grated	¼ – ½ teaspoon ground ginger

QUANTITIES PER HEAD

Appetizers	a variety of 4 - 6
Soup	5 servings to 1 quart
Sauces	10 servings to 1 pint
Fish	6 ozs. without bone
	8 ozs. with bone
Meat	4 ozs. without bone
	6 ozs. with bone
Green vegetables	6 servings 8 ozs.
Potatoes	4 servings 8 ozs.
Puddings/cold sweets	3 servings to 1 pint
Ices	10 servings to 1 quart
Poultry (chicken)	6 portions from a 4 lb. chicken
Poussin (chicken 3 - 4 weeks old)	1 portion

USEFUL KITCHEN EQUIPMENT

Cake tester	Blender
Poultry shears	Food chopper
Colander	Meat pounder
Rotary egg whisk	Nut grinder
Pastry blender	Pots, pans, casseroles
Pastry brush	Knives
Cheese graters	Sieves, rubber scrapers, bulb basters

Pots must be heavy bottomed. The best all purpose material is undoubtedly heavy enamelled cast iron. Copper pots are very satisfactory — the metal should be 1/8" thick and the handle should be of iron. A kitchen should have round and oval casseroles. Saucepans in various sizes — a skillet (sloping sides) and a saute pan (straight sides).

Omelette Pan — This can be made of iron, with a long handle and a 2" sloping side and a 7" diameter bottom. This is perfect for 2 — 3 egg omelettes. When new, scrub with steel wool and scouring powder. Rinse and dry. Heat it and rub bottom with oil and let it stand overnight. Just before using, sprinkle 1 teaspoon of salt in the pan and rub with a paper towel.

Knives must be good quality, and kept in good condition. A 9" blade for chopping vegetables, a pointed knife for filleting, which should have a 6½" flexible blade. Knives for splitting chickens should have a 12" blade and should be heavy.

A carver should only be used for carving.

INDEX

A

Ambrosia	59
Avocado & Grapefruit	35

B

Bahamian Conch Salad	37
Conch Soup	5
Mince Pie	63
Baked Bananas	64
Baked Black Crabs	11
Baked Cabbage	29
Baked Pork Chops	24
Baked Red Snapper	44
Baked Sweet Potato	34
Baking Powder Biscuits	67
Banana Bread	65
Banana King Fish with Mustard Sauce	11
Banana Meat Rolls	23
Banana Muffins	67
Bananas in Batter	59
Barbecues	
Bacon Wrapped Franks	44
Baked Red Snapper	44
Barbecued Chicken	45
Barbecued Chicken in Special Sauce	46
Barbecued Chicken Wings	45
Barbecued Lamb Chops	46
Barbecued Meat Balls	47
Barbecued Oriental Chicken	47
Barbecued Perch	47
Barbecued Spare Ribs	48
Barbecued Spare Ribs (Baked Style)	48
Barbecued Standing Ribs	49
Barbecued Steak	49
Beef Liver in Barbecue Sauce	49
Christmas Ham with Barbecue Sauce	50
Cooking Chart	44
Jiffy Barbecue Sauce	46
Orange Grilled Fish	50
Shrimp with Cold Barbecue Sauce	50
Smoked Pork Chops	50
Spicy Roast Beef Barbecue	51
Basic Bread Dough	65
Basic White Sauce	40
Beans in Sour Cream Sauce	28
Beef and Mango in Beer	22
Beef Curry with Green Bananas	22
Beef and Rice Casserole	26
Beet Soup	6
Beet with Orange Sauce	31
Biscuits - Dough	23
Blender Grapefruit Marmalade	58
Boiled Crawfish	10
Boiled Fish	10
Braised Duckling	19

Brawn	26
Breads — See Cakes & Breads	
Bread & Butter Pickles	52
Breadfruit Chips	4
Breadfruit Salad	36
Broad Bean Cutlets	28
Broad Bean Salad	35

C

Callaloo Bake	29
Callaloo Salad	36
Calf's Foot Jelly	57
Carrot Ambrosia	30
Carrot & Raisin Salad	36
Cauliflower Custard	30
Chicken Bahamas	16
Chicken Casserole	21
Chicken Orange	18
Chicken and Rice	16
Chicken Salad	37
Chicken Souse	16
Christmas Citrus Punch	73
Cho Chos Baked with Cheese	30
Cho Cho Salad	37
Chocolate Mousse	61
Cockerel Soup	6
Coconut Bread	68
Coconut Chips	2
Coconut Cookies	70
Coconut Cream Pie	60
Coconut Gizzadas	60
Coconut Loaf Cake	74
Coconut Mould	61
Coconut Trifle	60
Cod Fish Twice Laid	13
Coffee Mousse	65
Cold Thick Cucumber Soup	5
Conch Fritters	10
Conch Rice	32
Conch Salad	39
Conch Soup	35
Cooked Dressing	40
Cookies — See Cakes & Breads	
Cooking & Household Hints	80
Corn Relish	52
Cow Peas Soup	8
Crab Fritters	12
Crab Soup	6
Cracked Conch	14
Crawfish Bits	3
Crawfish Curry	1
Crawfish Soup	8
Crawfish Dip	4

Crawfish Fritters	3
Crawfish Newburg	13
Crawfish and Rice	15
Crawfish Salad	38
Crawfish Thermidor	14
Creamed Conch	14
Cucumber & Sour Cream Salad	37
Curried Lobster	15

D

Devil's Sauce	42
Different Stuffing for Roasted Chicken	17
Dressing for Seafood	41
Duck & Pineapple	20

E

Egg Bread	66
Egg Plant Elegante	1
Egg Plant with Cheese & Tomatoes	34
Egg Sauce	42
Escoveitch of Fish	12

F

Fish Chowder	7
Food Substitutions	88
Fried Plantain Chips	2
Fried Crawfish	13
Fruited Cabbage	29
Fruity Callaloo	30

G

Garlic Vinegar	54
Glossary of Cooking Terms	78
Grapefruit with Shrimp & Sour Cream	2
Grouper Pan Fried	15
Guava Butter	58
Guava Cheese	58
Guava Duff	63
Guava Jelly	57
Guava Jelly Cookies	70
Guava Layer Cake	69
Guava Mousse	62
Guava Pie	62
Gungu or Cow Peas Soup	7

H

Herb Vinegars	55
Honey Dressing for Fruit Salad	40
Hors D'oeuvres — See Appetizers & Hors D'oeuvres	
Hot Coconut Bread	68
Hot Dressing	40
Hot Pepper Sauce	42
Hot Pepper & Shallots	53

I

Island Fish Tea	7

J

Jamaica Bun	68
Jams — See Jellys & Jams	
Johnny Cake	67
Journey Cake	68

K

King Fish in Coconut Cream	12
Kitchen Equipments	83

L

Lime Pie	62
Liver with Sweet Peppers	25
Lobster Creole	13
Lobster Salad	38

M

Macaroni & Cheese	33
Mango Chutney	53
Mango Fool	67
Mango Pie	63
Marinated Pork Chops	27
Marina Sauce	42
Marmalade Sauce	42
Matrimony	71
Menus	74
Brunch	74
Lunch	75
Dinner	77
Mint Glazed Carrots	30
Mutton Stew	24
My Salad Dressing	41

N

Naseberry Nectar	71
Nassau Cake	3
Nassau Chicken	21
Nassau Chop Suey	27

O

Oil & Vinegar Dressing	41
Okra and Rice	31
Okra with Tomatoes	33
Okra Soup	5
Onion Salad	38
Orange Bread	66
Orange Cake	69
Orange Jelly	57
Orange Marmalade	58
Orange Sorbet	64
Oven Fried Fish	12
Oysters	1

P

Paw Paw Soup	8

Pan Fried Grouper Fingers	15
Peanut Sauce	43
Peas and Grits	33
Peas and Rice	32
Peppermint Sauce	43
Pepper Pot	8
Pepper Shrimps	3
Pepper Wine	55
Pickled Watermelon	54
Pie Crust	18
Pigeon Pie	18
Pigeon Peas Soup	9
Pigeons with Cabbage	18
Pigeons with Pineapple	19
Pineapple Appetizer	2
Pineapple Jam	56
Plantation Rum Punch	71
Pork Chops with Ginger Ale	25
Pork Chops with Pineapple	25
Pork Rind	2
Preserves — See Pickles & Preserves	
Pumpkin Bread	66
Pumpkin Jam	56
Pumpkin Pie	61
Pumpkin Puff	34
Pumpkin Soup	8

Q

Quantities Per Head	83
Quick Conch Salad	35

R

Rabbit Fricassee	26
Red Devil	53
Rice & Pumpkin	31
Ripe Banana Pie	59
Roasted Pigeon with Rice Stuffing	19
Rum Cake	69
Rum Coffee Jelly	64
Rum Sauce	43
Rump Steak Casserole	24

S

Sabayon Sauce	43
Salad Creole	39
Salmi of Duck	20
Salted Beef & Banana Casserole	22
Sauces — See Dressings & Sauces	
Sea Grape Jelly	57
Seasoned Breadfruit Chips	4

Shellfish — See Fish & Shellfish	
Shell Fish Curry	11
Shrimp Salad with Coconut Cream	39
Shrimp with Pineapple	15
Soda Bread	67
Sorrel Appetizer	72
Soursop Punch	72
Souse	23
Spiced Bahamian Souse	26
Spicy Dressing	41
Split Pea Soup	7
Starapple Appetizer	72
Steamed Crawfish	13
Steamed Wild Hog	25
String Bean Salad	36
Stuffed Breadfruit	29
Stuffed Chicken	17
Stuffed Paw Paw	34
Surprise Turtle Soup	9
Sunday Chicken	17
Sweet & Sour Sauce	43
Sweet Pepper Salad	38
Sweet Potato Cookies	70

T

Table of Measurements	82
Tasty Low Cholestrol Recipe for Pastry	69
Three Bean Salad	36
Tomato Jam	56
To Preserve Fresh Tomatoes	53
Tropical Chicken	17
Tropical Fruit Salad	61
Tropical Salad	39
Turtle Soup Clear	9
Turtle Soup Thick	9
Two Minute Mayonnaise	41

V

Vegetable Relish	54

W

Watermelon Marbles	4
Whelk Soup	6
White Crown Pigeon	20
White Sauce	14

Y

Yam Casserole	34